ARTILLERY

OF WORLD WAR II

ARTILLERY

OF WORLD WAR II

Chris Chant

MBI Publishing
Company

This edition first published in 2001 by MBI Publishing
Company, Galtier Plaza, Suite 200
380 Jackson Street, St. Paul, MN 55101-3885 USA

MBI Publishing Company books are also available at discounts in
bulk quantity for industrial or sales-promotional use. For details
write to Special Sales Manager at Motorbooks International
Wholesalers & Distributors, Galtier Plaza, Suite 200
380 Jackson Street, St. Paul, MN 55101-3885 USA

Library of Congress Cataloging-in-Publication Data Available.

ISBN 0-7603-1172-2

Printed in Hong Kong

Editorial and design
Brown Partworks Limited
8 Chapel Place
Rivington Street
London
EC2A 3DQ
UK

Editor: Anne Cree
Picture research: Antony Shaw
Design: Jeni Child
Production: Matt Weyland

Printed in Hong Kong

CONTENTS

CANON DE 47

SPECIFICATIONS

CANON DE 47

Type:
light towed AT gun

Calibre:
47mm (1.85in)

Vehicle length:
n/a

Length of barrel:
2.49m (98in)

Weight travelling:
n/a

Weight in action:
1070kg (2360lb)

Elevation arc:
-13° to +16.5°

Traverse arc:
68°

Effective ceiling:
n/a

Road range:
n/a

Range:
unknown

Projectile weight:
1.725kg (3.8lb)

Armour:
n/a

Engine:
n/a

Muzzle velocity:
855mps (2805fps)

Speed:
n/a

The two smallest-calibre towed anti-tank guns operated by the French at the beginning of World War II were the 25mm Canon léger de 25 antichar SA-L modèles 1934 and 1937, these being L/72 and L/77 weapons respectively. Both weapons were too lightly built and possessed only indifferent armour-penetration capability, but the same cannot be said of the two weapons next up the calibre ladder. These were the 47mm SA modèle 1937 APX and the later but virtually identical SA modèle 1939 APX, which were both sturdy and capable weapons. Low to the ground and comparatively easy to handle, both weapons could have played a major part in the campaign of 1940 had they been given the opportunity. Germany seized large numbers of these guns, and pressed them into service by its occupation forces right into the time of the Allied invasion of 1944.

In German service the modèles 1937 and 1939 became the 4.7cm PaK 181(f) and PaK 183(f) respectively, and moderately large numbers of the weapons were also used in self-propelled anti-tank mountings including the 4.7cm PaK 181(f) oder 183(f) auf PzJäg Lorraine Schlepper(f), the 4.7cm PaK(f) auf Panzerspähwagen P204(f), the 4.7cm PaK(f) auf Infanterie PzKpfw Mk II(e), and the 4.7cm Pak 181(f) oder 183(f) auf PzKpfw 35R(f).

CANON DE 75 1897

The Canon de 75 modèle 1897 can lay claim to being the progenitor of modern quick-firing artillery and was also the most extensively fielded light gun ever placed in service. Produced by Schneider from 1897, the "75" was the first modern field piece as it employed the first successful hydraulic recoil system, while the Nordenfeld breech block allowed a high rate of fire. Before 1914 the gun was one of the most closely guarded French secrets, but by 1918 was used by many countries. As late as 1939 the "75" was still in widespread service. The USA fielded the gun in M1897A2 and A4 variants up to 1941. Poland used the type as the armata polowa wt 1897 or wt 97/17, and in 1939 and 1940 the British Army received small numbers with the designation Ordnance, QF, 75mm Mk I. The gun still served with the Romanian and Greek armies, and some delivered to Lithuania passed into service with the Red Army. By 1939 many of the French guns, of which several thousands were still in service, had been modernized with pneumatic tyres, but large numbers with the original pattern of wooden spoked wheels remained in service. After France's June 1940 defeat many equipments fell into German hands to receive the designation FK 231(f) but more common designation FK 97(f). In 1942 they converted some 600 barrels for use as PaK 97/38 and 97/40 anti-tank guns.

SPECIFICATIONS

CANON DE 75 1897

Type: **light towed field gun**	Effective ceiling: **n/a**
Calibre: **75mm (2.95in)**	Road range: **n/a**
Vehicle length: **n/a**	Range: **11,100m (12,140 yards)**
Length of barrel: **2.587m (101.85in)**	Projectile weight: **6.195kg (13.66lb)**
Weight travelling: **1970kg (4344lb)**	Armour: **n/a**
Weight in action: **1140kg (2514lb)**	Engine: **n/a**
Elevation arc: **-11° to +18°**	Muzzle velocity: **575mps (1886fps)**
Traverse arc: **6°**	Speed: **n/a**

CANON DE 75 1933

SPECIFICATIONS

CANON DE 75 1933

Type:
  medium AA gun

Effective ceiling:
  7200m (23,620ft)

Calibre:
  75mm (2.95in)

Road range:
  n/a

Vehicle length:
  n/a

Range:
  n/a

Length of barrel:
  4m (157in)

Projectile weight:
  9kg (19.85lb)

Weight travelling:
  n/a

Armour:
  n/a

Weight in action:
  4200kg (9259lb)

Engine:
  n/a

Elevation arc:
  0° to +70°

Muzzle velocity:
  715mps (2346fps)

Traverse arc:
  360°

Speed:
  n/a

Like many French artillery pieces in service on the outbreak of World War II, the Canon de 75 contre aeronefs sur remorque Schneider had its origins in World War I, specifically the Canon de 75 anti-aérien modèle 1917 sur plate-forme Schneider using the barrel of the modèle 1897 field gun. In an effort to update the weapon, the original barrel was replaced in 1934 by a more modern barrel and the heavy carriage was retained in an updated form and fitted with a complex fire-control system. In 1940 many of these Canon de 75 contre aeronefs modèle 1917/34 sur remorque Schneider were seized by the Germans and kept in service with the revised designation 7.5cm FlaK M.17/34(f). The Canon de 75 contre aeronefs modèle 1930 was basically similar but lacked the on-carriage fire-control system, as a central predictor was employed. The Germans used this gun as the 7.5cm FlaK M.30(f). The Canon de 75 contre aeronefs modèle 1933 represented an effort to modernize the 75mm family of AA guns by installing the modified Schneider barrel on a more modern mounting: a folding cruciform with a conventional pedestal and folding platform for the detachment of one commander and 10 men. Only limited numbers were produced, the Germans taking these for service as the 7.5cm FlaK M.33(f) weapons.

CANON DE 105 C

Early in the 1930s the French Army realized that it needed heavier field artillery than the 75mm modèle 1897 rapid-fire gun, which was now an obsolescent piece of artillery that should be replaced by a type or types of more modern design and offering the ability to deliver heavier fire to a longer range.

The first result of this process was an order placed with the Schneider armaments company for a field howitzer in 105mm rather than 75mm calibre. The resulting Canon de 105 C modèle 1934 Schneider (specification at right) was of conventional design without any genuinely distinctive features, and had split trails, a large and angular gun, and large-diameter spoked wheels with solid rubber tyres providing the capability for motor traction at a comparatively high speed.

Trials of the weapon were completed without undue problem, though this was due to its adequate design and lack of any radical features, and production was then started without delay; this helped to ensure that the French Army had moderately large numbers of these pieces in service in 1939 to meet the expected German Army invasion. Following the defeat of France in June 1940 many were captured by the German Army for service and given the designation 10.5cm leichte Feldhaubitze 324(f).

SPECIFICATIONS

CANON DE 105 C

Type: **medium towed howitzer**	Effective ceiling: **n/a**
Calibre: **105mm (4.13in)**	Road range: **n/a**
Vehicle length: **n/a**	Range: **10,300m (11,265 yards)**
Length of barrel: **1.95m (76.7in)**	Projectile weight: **15.6kg (34.4lb)**
Weight travelling: **unknown**	Armour: **n/a**
Weight in action: **1722kg (3797lb)**	Engine: **n/a**
Elevation arc: **-8° to +50°**	Muzzle velocity: **440mps (1444fps)**
Traverse arc: **58°**	Speed: **n/a**

CANON DE 155C

SPECIFICATIONS

CANON DE 155C

Type: **heavy gun/howitzer**	Effective ceiling: **n/a**
Calibre: **155mm (6.1in)**	Road range: **n/a**
Vehicle length: **n/a**	Range: **11,300m (12,360 yards)**
Length of barrel: **2.176mm (85.67in)**	Projectile weight: **43.61kg (96.16lb)**
Weight travelling: **3720kg (8203lb)**	Armour: **n/a**
Weight in action: **3300kg (7277lb)**	Engine: **n/a**
Elevation arc: **0° to +42° 20'**	Muzzle velocity: **450mps (1476fps)**
Traverse arc: **6°**	Speed: **n/a**

The nature and intensity of the warfare fought on the Western Front during World War I demanded weapons tailored to the particular demands of essentially static fighting, and one French result was the Canon de 155 C modèle 1917, generally known as the C 17 S.

This weapon entered service in 1917 and soon gained an excellent reputation, being adopted for US service as the 155mm Howitzer M1917 and M1917A1, and after World War I was also exported to many nations including Brazil, Finland, Romania and Yugoslavia. As a result the weapon was still in widespread service during 1939, in which France could still muster more than 2000 such equipments in frontline roles. The Soviet guns had been sleeved in the Soviet 152mm calibre, and all the weapons captured by the Germans from the Soviets after the invasion of June 1941 and other conquered countries were pressed into service in tasks as diverse as standard field use and coastal defence.

The ex-Belgian Obusier de 155 became the 15.5cm schwere Feldhaubitze 413(b), the French C 17 S became the 15.5cm sFH 414(f), the Italian Obice da 155/14 PB became the 15.5cm sFH 414(i), the Polish 155mm haubica wz 1917 became the 15.5cm sFH 17(p) and the Soviet 152-17S became the 15.2cm sFH 449(r). It was certainly a reliable and robust weapon.

CANON DE 155 GRAND PUISSANCE

The Canon de 155 Grand Puissance Filloux (GPF) entered service in 1917 and, proving itself one of the best pieces of French artillery in World War I, was chosen for use by the US Army forces in France during 1918. The type remained in American service into World War II as the 155mm Gun M1918M1.

There were still some 450 GPF equipments in French service during 1939, and after June 1940 the Germans used seized weapons with the designation 15.5cm Kanone 418(f) in the field and coastal defence roles. The Canon de 155 Grand Puissance Filloux - CA was a development of the GPF firing a different type of ammunition from a revised chamber. Only a few such equipments were still in service during 1939, and captured examples were not taken into German service for field use as their capabilities were inferior to those of the GPF. Statically emplaced GPF-CA weapons were retained with the designation 15.5cm K 417(f) until all ammunition had been used (these weapons were of little use, but looked good for newsreels to boost civilian morale). The canon de 155 Grand Puissance Filloux - Touzzard was a modernized GPF with a new carriage carried on six pneumatically tyred wheels of which two were removed as the gun was brought into action. The GPF-T was operated by the Germans as the 15.5cm K 419(f).

SPECIFICATIONS

CANON DE 155 G.P.

Type: **heavy towed gun**	Effective ceiling: **n/a**
Calibre: **155mm (6.1in)**	Road range: **n/a**
Vehicle length: **n/a**	Range: **19,500m (21,325 yards)**
Length of barrel: **5.725m (225.4in)**	Projectile weight: **43kg (94.8lb)**
Weight travelling: **11,700kg (25,794lb)**	Armour: **n/a**
Weight in action: **10,750kg (23,700lb)**	Engine: **n/a**
Elevation arc: **0° to +35°**	Muzzle velocity: **735mps (2411fps)**
Traverse arc: **60°**	Speed: **n/a**

CANON DE 155 1932

SPECIFICATIONS

CANON DE 155 1932

Type: **heavy howitzer**	Effective ceiling: **n/a**
Calibre: **155mm (6.1in)**	Road range: **n/a**
Vehicle length: **n/a**	Range: **27,500m (30,075 yards)**
Length of barrel: **8.525m (335.6in)**	Projectile weight: **50kg (110lb)**
Weight travelling: **n/a**	Armour: **n/a**
Weight in action: **16,400kg (36,155lb)**	Engine: **n/a**
Elevation arc: **-8° to +45°**	Muzzle velocity: **900mps (2953fps)**
Traverse arc: **360°**	Speed: **n/a**

A characteristic of the guns and howitzers developed for service with the French Army in the period before and during World War I had been their comparatively short range. This was not perceived as being a tactical limitation during the first half of the 1920s, but by the second half of the decade the armies of the larger European countries were beginning to develop concepts of fast-moving mobile warfare based on motorization if not mechanization of their forces. This type of warfare clearly required that infantry and armoured forces should be provided with artillery support firing at longer ranges, and the French Army therefore called for a new generation of weapons capable of motorized towing at higher speed and of firing a heavier projectile to a longer range. An immediate result of this demand was the Canon 155 L modèle 32 Schneider. This was an orthodox but thoroughly modern piece of artillery by the standards of the day, and its two most obvious tactical capabilities were accuracy to a long range and an advanced mounting and carriage offering the capacity for high-speed towing and, after the gun had been emplaced, 360° traverse. The gun proved useful in the campaign of May–June 1940, and after the defeat of France the surviving equipments were seized by the Germans.

FLAK 38

The capability of the FlaK 30 was hampered by the gun's low rate of fire, so Mauser was allocated the task of boosting the firing rate and, at the same time, significantly reducing the gun's tendency to jam. The result was the 2cm Flak 38 that appeared in 1940 with a revised breech mechanism improving the cyclic and practical rates of fire to 420–480 and 180–220rpm respectively. The feed system and carriage/trailer were essentially unaltered, but sighting was now effected by means of the Flakvisier 38, a complex and somewhat fragile and expensive unit replaced from 1941 by the Linealvisier 38 open ring sight, itself succeeded from a time late in 1944 by the Schwebekreisvisier 38.

The FlaK 38 supplemented but did not supplant the FlaK 30, and during August 1944 the German air force alone had in service just under 17,600 Flak 30 and FlaK 38 guns. The FlaK 38 used the same ammunition as the Flak 30 and had the same detachment, and was also carried on a number of self-propelled mountings including the leichte Selbstfahrlafette (2cm FlaK 38) (SdKfz 10/5), the 2cm Flak 38 auf Mannschaftkraftwagen, the 2cm FlaK 38 auf le gl Lkw Kfz 70, the mittlerer Schützenpanzerwagen (2cm FlaK 38) (SdKfz 251), the SdKfz 251/17, and the leichte Flakpanzer 18(t) (SdKfz 140).

SPECIFICATIONS

FLAK 38

Type: **light towed AA gun**	Effective ceiling: **2200m (6630ft)**
Calibre: **20mm (0.8in)**	Road range: **n/a**
Vehicle length: **n/a**	Range: **n/a**
Length of barrel: **2.2525m (88.68in)**	Projectile weight: **0.119kg (0.2625lb)**
Weight travelling: **750kg (1,654lb)**	Armour: **n/a**
Weight in action: **420kg (926lb)**	Engine: **n/a**
Elevation arc: **-20° to +90°**	Muzzle velocity: **900mps (2953fps)**
Traverse arc: **360°**	Speed: **n/a**

FLAKVIERLING 38

SPECIFICATIONS

FLAKVIERLING 38

Type: **light towed AA gun**	Effective ceiling: **2200m (7220ft)**
Calibre: **20mm (0.8in)**	Road range: **n/a**
Vehicle length: **n/a**	Range: **n/a**
Length of barrel: **2.252m (88.7in)**	Projectile weight: **0.119kg (0.2625lb)**
Weight travelling: **2212kg (4877lb)**	Armour: **n/a**
Weight in action: **1514kg (3338lb)**	Engine: **n/a**
Elevation arc: **-10° to +100°**	Muzzle velocity: **900mps (2953fps)**
Traverse arc: **360°**	Speed: **n/a**

The 2cm Flakvierling 38 quadruple 20mm mounting was highly respected by Allied airmen operating at low level. Designed by Mauser for German naval use, the Flakvierling 38 entered production for the army and air force during 1940. The Flakvierling 38 combined four FlaK 38 barrels on an adapted version of the FlaK 38's carriage, and while the standard sight was the Flakvisier 40 or improved Flakvisier 40A, provision was being made for radar direction by the end of World War II.

The need to keep four barrels supplied with ammunition meant that the detachment was increased to a commander and seven men (reduced to six from August 1944) rather than the FlaK 38's total of six men: this provided for four loading and ammunition numbers in place of the FlaK 38's two, but the Flakvierling 38 could be operated by just four men.

The Flakvierling 38 was carried on trains and installed on FlaK towers to supplement heavier weapons, and was also used on a number of self-propelled mountings including the 2cm Flakvierling 38 auf m Lkw, the mittlerer Zugkraftwagen 8t mit 2cm Flakvierling 38 (SdKfz 7/1), the Flakpanzer IV (2cm Flakvierling 38) auf Fgst PzKpfw IV Möbelwagen, and the Flakpanzer IV (2cm) auf Fgst PzKpfw IV/3 Wirbelwind. It was an excellent and reliable weapon.

FLAKPANZER IV

There were two Flakpanzer IV types, namely the Flakpanzer IV (2cm Flakvierling 38) auf Fgst PzKpfw IV Möbelwagen (furniture van) and the Flakpanzer IV (2cm) mit PzFgst Panzer IV/3 Wirbelwind (whirlwind). The former was developed as the Flakpanzer 38(t), with one 20mm FlaK 38 cannon on a Czechoslovak light tank chassis, and had not proved satisfactory, and the new type entered production in 1943.

The Möbelwagen comprised a Flakvierling 38 four-gun mounting (provided with 3000 rounds) on a PzKpfw IV medium tank chassis. A large rectangular fighting compartment of armour plate was provided above the superstructure for protection, and in action this compartment's walls were lowered to the horizontal position to enlarge the fighting platform. The gun mounting could be traversed through 360° and elevated in an arc from +10° to +90°. The Flakpanzer IV (2cm) mit PzFgst Panzer IV/3 was introduced at the end of 1943 after being designed to provide better protection to the gun crew through the installation of the Flakvierling 38 (with 3200 rounds) in an open-topped octagonal rotating armoured turret that could be rotated through 360° and provided the gun mounting with an elevation arc between +10° and +90°. The specification applies to the Wirbelwind.

SPECIFICATIONS

FLAKPANZER IV

Type: **self-propelled AA gun**	Effective ceiling: **n/a**
Calibre: **n/a**	Road range: **210km (130 miles)**
Vehicle length: **5.89m (19ft 4in)**	Range: **n/a**
Length of barrel: **n/a**	Projectile weight: **n/a**
Weight travelling: **n/a**	Armour: **16–85mm (.6–3.35in)**
Weight in action: **22,176kg (48,889lb)**	Engine: **Maybach HL 120 TR 112**
Elevation arc: **n/a**	Muzzle velocity: **n/a**
Traverse arc: **n/a**	Speed: **40km/h (24.8mph)**

FLAKPANZER WIRBELWIND

SPECIFICATIONS

FLAKPANZER WIRBELWIND

Type:
self-propelled AA gun

Effective ceiling:
n/a

Calibre:
n/a

Road range:
210km (130 miles)

Vehicle length:
5.89m (19ft 4in)

Range:
n/a

Length of barrel:
n/a

Projectile weight:
n/a

Weight travelling:
n/a

Armour:
16–85mm (.63–3.35in)

Weight in action:
22,175kg (48,887lb)

Engine:
Maybach HL 120 TR 112

Elevation arc:
n/a

Muzzle velocity:
n/a

Traverse arc:
n/a

Speed:
n/a

A tactically important weapon that entered service in December 1943 to provide German armoured forces with a high level of air defence against low-flying attack aircraft, the five-man Flakpanzer IV (2cm) mit PzFgst Panzer IV/3 Wirbelwind (whirlwind) was based on the chassis of the PzKpfw IV Ausf J medium tank. This ensured that the vehicle had mobility equal to the battle tanks then in service, while the design of the armament installation ensured that the gun crew had better protection than had been offered in earlier self-propelled anti-aircraft gun mountings. This protection was created by the installation of the 2cm Flakvierling 38 unit, with its four 20mm cannon, inside an eight-sided turret, with outward-angled lower sides and inward-angled upper sides of exactly the same dimensions to facilitate the task of welding together the turret's 16mm (0.63in) plates. The turret had power traverse through 360°, and the guns could be elevated through an arc between +10° and +90°. Ammunition for the guns was carried in 20-round clips, stowage being provided for 16 such clips in the turret for replenishment from some 2280 more rounds carried in 15 boxes inside the hull. The Flakpanzer IV (3.7cm) Ostwind (east wind) was basically similar except for its armament of one 3.7cm Flak 43 gun in a turret.

FLAK 36/37

Production of Germany's first modern light anti-aircraft gun, the FlaK 18, ended in 1936 to allow manufacture of an improved model, the 3.7cm FlaK 36, that was the FlaK 18 gun on a new mounting carried on a two-wheeled carriage and served by an eight-man detachment. The ballistics of the FlaK 36 were the same as those of the FlaK 18 but when, in 1940, there appeared a new range of ammunition characterized by one rather than the original two driving bands, the FlaK 36's chamber was shortened accordingly. The FlaK 36 was originally sighted with the aid of the Flakvisier 35 or 36 until Zeiss developed its clockwork-powered Uhrwerksvisier that was accepted for service as the Flakvisier 37.

Equipments fitted with this sight were FlaK 37, and were in all other respects identical to the FlaK 36. The FlaK 36 and 37 became the German forces' standard defence against low-flying warplanes, and were used in 9- or 12-gun batteries by the land-based forces. The weapons were also fitted on trains, surface warships, U-boats, FlaK towers and a number of self-propelled mountings to create the 3.7cm FlaK auf Lkw Mercedes-Benz 4500 A, the 3.7cm FlaK auf Maultier, the 3.7cm FlaK (Sf) auf Zugkraftwagen 5t SdKfz 6/2, and the mZgkw 8t mit 3.7cm Flak 36 SdKfz 7/2.

SPECIFICATIONS

FLAK 36/37

Type:
light towed AA gun

Calibre:
37mm (1.457in)

Vehicle length:
n/a

Length of barrel:
3.626m (142.75in)

Weight travelling:
2400kg (5291lb)

Weight in action:
1550kg (3417lb)

Elevation arc:
-8° to +85°

Traverse arc:
360°

Effective ceiling:
4800m (15,750ft)

Road range:
n/a

Range:
n/a

Projectile weight:
0.64kg (1.4lb)

Armour:
n/a

Engine:
n/a

Muzzle velocity:
820mps (2690fps)

Speed:
n/a

PAK 35/36

SPECIFICATIONS

PAK 35/36

Type:
towed light AT gun

Calibre:
37mm (1.46in)

Vehicle length:
n/a

Length of barrel:
1.665m (65.5in)

Weight travelling:
432kg (952lb)

Weight in action:
328kg (723lb)

Elevation arc:
-8° to +25°

Traverse arc:
60°

Effective ceiling:
n/a

Road range:
n/a

Range:
375m (410 yards)

Projectile weight:
0.354kg (12.5oz)

Armour:
n/a

Engine:
n/a

Muzzle velocity:
1030mps (3379fps)

Speed:
n/a

The 3.7cm PaK 35/36 entered service in 1936. More than 15,000 such weapons had been completed in Germany by 1941, and the type was also built under licence by other countries. Experience proved that by the standards of the day the PaK 35/36 was excellent, and the weapon strongly influenced the design of other guns: the American 37mm M3, for example, was a close copy. By the end of 1940 it was clear that the PaK 35/36 was obsolescent in the face of thicker tank armour, and the weapon was gradually replaced by larger-calibre guns. In the shorter term the effectiveness of the PaK 35/36 was boosted by tungsten-cored AP40 ammunition, and in secondary battlefield roles the PaK 35/36 remained in service to the end of World War II.

It was also used by other countries that later fell to Germany in the war. Thus the Soviet 37mm Anti-Tank Gun Model 1930 became the PaK 158(r), the Italian Cannone contracarro da 37/45 became the PaK 162(i), and the Dutch 37mm Rheinmetall became the PaK 153(h). Self-propelled mountings of the PaK 35/36 included the 3.7cm PaK auf I ge Lkw(o), 3.7cm PaK auf Fahrgestell Bren(e), the 3.7cm PaK (Sf) auf Infanterie Schlepper UE(f), the 3.7cm PaK auf gep Artillerieschlepper(r), the 3.7cm Pak auf le Zgkw and the 3.7cm PaK (Sf) auf Zgkw 1t.

PAK 38

The need for an anti-tank gun with a calibre greater than that of the 3.7cm PaK 35/36 had been anticipated even as the PaK 35/36 was entering service, and the design of a new 5cm weapon began during 1938. The design authority was again Rheinmetall-Borsig, and the new weapon entered service late in 1940 as the 5cm Panzerabwehrkanone 38. This was a capable gun that remained in service right to the end of World War II: firing tungsten-cored AP40 ammunition, the PaK 38 could successfully tackle all but the most heavily protected Allied tanks, and between 1941 and 1942 was the only German anti-tank gun able to penetrate the armour of the Soviet T-34 tank.

The employment of light alloys in the carriage lighted the equipment and made it easier to handle. The wheels had torsion-bar suspension that was locked when the trails were split, creating a stable firing platform. Later in the war the PaK 38 was adapted for aircraft mounting as the Bordkanone 5 with an automatic feed system, and this was then used as the basis for the 5cm FlaK 214 anti-aircraft gun. As an anti-tank gun the PaK 38 was installed on a number of self-propelled mountings including the 5cm PaK 38 (Sf) auf leichter Selbstfahrlafette, the SdKfz 250 and the 5cm Pak 38 auf PzKpfw II nA.

SPECIFICATIONS

PAK 38

Type: **medium towed AT gun**	Effective ceiling: **n/a**
Calibre: **50mm (1.97in)**	Road range: **n/a**
Vehicle length: **n/a**	Range: **450m (490 yards)**
Length of barrel: **3.173m (124.9in)**	Projectile weight: **2.25kg (4lb 15.25oz)**
Weight travelling: **986kg (2174lb)**	Armour: **n/a**
Weight in action: **unknown**	Engine: **n/a**
Elevation arc: **-8° to +27°**	Muzzle velocity: **1198mps (3930fps)**
Traverse arc: **65°**	Speed: **n/a**

LE IG 18

SPECIFICATIONS

LE IG 18

Type:
infantry support gun

Effective ceiling:
n/a

Calibre:
75mm (2.95in)

Road range:
n/a

Vehicle length:
n/a

Range:
3550m (3885 yards)

Length of barrel:
0.884m (34.8in)

Projectile weight:
6–5.45kg (13.2–12lb)

Weight travelling:
unknown

Armour:
n/a

Weight in action:
400kg (882lb)

Engine:
n/a

Elevation arc:
-10° to +73°

Muzzle velocity:
210mps (689fps)

Traverse arc:
12°

Speed:
n/a

One of the pieces of light field artillery used in the largest numbers by the German Army in World War II was the 7.5cm leichte Infanteriegeschütz 18. The need for such a weapon was perceived in the first half of the 1920s, and the task of designing and developing such a gun was entrusted to Rheinmetall during 1927. Field trials of the new equipment proved very successful, and a major manufacturing programme was initiated so that the le IG 18 could be adopted as the standard artillery weapon of the support companies of infantry regiments and also of some mountain units. The le IG 18 featured an unusual loading system in which the barrel was wholly enclosed in a square slipper which pivoted upwards as the breech block remained fixed. Early examples of the le IG 18 had old-fashioned spoked wheels better suited to horse traction, but later equipments ran on pneumatically tyred wheels of the type required for higher-speed towing behind motor vehicles. A special variant, produced in 1939 to the extent of just six equipments, was the 7.5cm le IG 18F (Fallschirmjäger, or airborne forces), which was intended for paradropping for the support of airborne forces: this model had small wheels, lacked any shield and could be broken down into four 140kg (309lb) loads carried in containers. Another limited-production variant was the 7.5cm le GebIG 18.

GEBIRGS-GESCHÜTZ 36

It was in 1935 that Rheinmetall-Borsig, working on the basis of a requirement issued by the German Army, embarked on the process of developing a new piece of thoroughly modern light artillery for service with Germany's mountain infantry formations. The new gun/howitzer was to become the standard gun of the artillery batteries supporting such infantry and was, of course, to be of the pack type so that the entire weapon could be broken down into loads which could each be carried by a draft animal, most typically a mule. The resulting weapon entered service in 1938 as the 7.5cm Gebirgsgeschütz 36, whose unusual features included variable recoil facility and a large muzzle brake of the pepperpot type. The Gebirgsgeschütz 36 could be broken down into eight loads, but service use soon revealed that the weapon was decidedly heavy for its role. Even so, the weapon proved popular with the men of batteries operating it as it was generally easy to handle and offered considerable stability when fired. The replacement for the Gebirgsgeschütz 36 was to have been the Gebirgsgeschütz 43 of the same calibre, for which Rheinmetall and Bohler offered designs. The Bohler design was preferred, but as only four were completed the Gebirgsgeschütz 36 remained in service to the end of World War II.

SPECIFICATIONS

GEBIRGSGESCHÜTZ 36

Type: **light mountain gun**	Effective ceiling: **n/a**
Calibre: **75mm (2.95in)**	Road range: **n/a**
Vehicle length: **n/a**	Range: **9150m (10,390 yards)**
Length of barrel: **1.4475m (57in)**	Projectile weight: **5.83kg (12.85lb)**
Weight travelling: **unknown**	Armour: **n/a**
Weight in action: **750kg (1653lb)**	Engine: **n/a**
Elevation arc: **-10° to +70°**	Muzzle velocity: **475mps (1558fps)**
Traverse arc: **40°**	Speed: **n/a**

FELDKANONE 38

SPECIFICATIONS

FELDKANONE 38

Type: light towed gun	**Effective ceiling:** n/a
Calibre: 75mm (2.95in)	**Road range:** n/a
Vehicle length: n/a	**Range:** 11,500m (12,575 yards)
Length of barrel: 2.335m (91.9in)	**Projectile weight:** 5.83kg (12.85lb)
Weight travelling: 1860kg (4101lb)	**Armour:** n/a
Weight in action: 1365 kg (3,009lb)	**Engine:** n/a
Elevation arc: -5° to +45°	**Muzzle velocity:** 605mps (1985fps)
Traverse arc: 50°	**Speed:** n/a

A piece of light field artillery used by the German Army only to a limited degree, the 7.5cm Feldkanone 38 was based on a design created and manufactured by the arms manufacturer Krupp in response to an order from the Brazilian Army, which received 64 such equipments with six-baffle muzzle brakes and large-diameter spoked wooden wheels inside steel tyres (as shown).

During 1942 the Germany Army found itself in need of substantially larger quantities of more modern field artillery, largely to satisfy its needs on the Eastern Front against the masses of Soviet manpower and hardware, and as a result Krupp adapted its Brazilian design to create the 7.5cm Feldkanone 38 that was built to provide a partial replacement for the obsolete 7.5cm leichte Feldkanone, a Krupp weapon that entered service in 1931 and reflected World War I artillery thinking rather than the requirements of modern mobile warfare as was being practised over the vast distances on the Eastern Front. Features of the FK 38 were trail legs that were heavier and larger than those of the Brazilian weapon as well as a two-baffle muzzle brake and typically solid German wheels or steel construction with sold rubber types. Like most pieces of German field artillery, the FK 38 fired fixed (one-piece) ammunition.

PAK 41

Built in competition with the Rheinmetall-Borsig 7.5cm PaK 40 as a means of providing the German Army with the best possible weapon to succeed the 5cm PaK 35/36, the 7.5cm Panzerabwehrkanone 41 was designed by Krupp, the other main creator of larger-calibre weapons for the German Army. The weapon was characterized by the incorporation of several advanced features. The equipment was thus the largest of the Gerlich taper-bore guns with a calibre of 7.5cm at the breech reducing to 5.5cm at the muzzle. It possessed trail legs attached directly to the one-piece shield in a fashion that effected considerable economies in manufacturing time and also in weight, and incorporated an automatic hydraulic braking system operated by the towing vehicle. In addition, the PaK 41 had a commendably low overall silhouette, and its comparatively light weight was a decided advantage in handling the weapon. But for its particular ammunition requirement, which was based on a tungsten-cored shot with collapsing light alloy skirts, and a barrel that lasted for only 400 rounds because of the demands placed on it, the PaK 41 might well have become a standard weapon. Thus only 150 PaK 41 guns were produced, and when tungsten for their special ammunition was exhausted, the weapons were scrapped.

SPECIFICATIONS

PAK 41

Type: **medium towed AT gun**	Effective ceiling: **n/a**
Calibre: **75/55mm (2.95/2.1in)**	Road range: **n/a**
Vehicle length: **n/a**	Range: **n/a**
Length of barrel: **4.32m (170in)**	Projectile weight: **2.59kg (5lb 11.25oz)**
Weight travelling: **1356kg (2989lb)**	Armour: **n/a**
Weight in action: **unknown**	Engine: **n/a**
Elevation arc: **0° to +16°**	Muzzle velocity: **1124mps (3690fps)**
Traverse arc: **60°**	Speed: **n/a**

JAGDPANZER 38(T)

SPECIFICATIONS

JAGDPANZER 38(T)

Type:
four-man tank hunter

Effective ceiling:
n/a

Calibre:
n/a

Road range:
160km (99 miles)

Vehicle length:
6.27m (20ft 7in)

Range:
n/a

Length of barrel:
n/a

Projectile weight:
n/a

Weight travelling:
unknown

Armour:
8–60mm (.3–2.36in)

Weight in action:
15,925kg (35,108lb)

Engine:
one EPA TZJ

Elevation arc:
n/a

Muzzle velocity:
n/a

Traverse arc:
n/a

Speed:
25.75km/h (16mph)

Manufactured from 1943 to provide the German forces with a dedicated Panzerjäger (tank hunter) capable of defeating the Allied powers' latest armoured fighting vehicles, the Jagdpanzer 38(t) "Hetzer" (baiter) was based on the redesigned hull of the PzKpfw 38(t) light tank of Czechoslovak origins. The front, sides and rear of the superstructure were extended upward to a small horizontal roof by the acute inward-angling of the front, sides and rear to provide superior ballistic protection yet still providing a fighting compartment for the four-man crew. The lower part of the hull's front was 60mm (2.36in) thick, angled at 40°, and was interlocked with the sides and upper nose plate, the latter also 60mm thick but angled at 60° up to the top of the superstructure. The primary armament was one 7.5cm PaK 39 (L/48) gun located some 0.38m (15in) to the right of the hull centreline, and fitted with an improved type of recoil mechanism permitting the muzzle brake to be omitted. The PaK 39's elevation arc was -6° to +10° and its traverse arc was 11° right and 5° left of the centreline, and 41 rounds of ammunition were carried. One 7.92mm machine gun was supported on a mounting built into the roof and fitted with a periscopic sight and extended trigger mechanism. Production totalled 1577 vehicles.

JAGDPANZER IV

Introduced late in 1943, the Jagdpanzer IV was based on the PzKpfw IV medium tank with the turret removed and the upper hull revised into a fixed superstructure, including 60mm (2.47in) upper and lower frontal plates sloped at 45° and 57° respectively, above the all-welded original hull. The sloping sides of the superstructure extended beyond the vertical hull sides over the tracks to provide additional volume for ammunition stowage (a maximum of 79 rounds). Armour skirts of 5mm (0.2in) thickness were bolted to brackets welded to the vehicle's sides.

The 7.5cm Pak 39 L/48 main gun was installed in the sloped front plate, the mounting being of the gimbal type protected by a heavy external casting. The gun could be elevated between -8° and +10°, and traversed between 12° left and 10° right. The PaK 39 provided a muzzle velocity of 700m (2297ft) per second with APCBC ammunition and 550m (1805ft) per second HE ammunition, and there were also AP40 and smoke projectiles. On later models of the equipment the muzzle brake was omitted, together with the machine-gun port on the left side of the front plate. Potent on paper, this vehicle was unreliable and produced in too few numbers to make a real impact on the battlefield at a time when Germany desperately needed good kit.

SPECIFICATIONS

JAGDPANZER IV

Type: **four-man tank hunter**	Effective ceiling: **n/a**
Calibre: **n/a**	Road range: **220km (130 miles)**
Vehicle length: **7.29m (23ft 11in)**	Range: **n/a**
Length of barrel: **n/a**	Projectile weight: **n/a**
Weight travelling: **n/a**	Armour: **10–60mm (.3–2.36in)**
Weight in action: **23,788kg (52,443lb)**	Engine: **Maybach HL 120 TRM**
Elevation arc: **n/a**	Muzzle velocity: **n/a**
Traverse arc: **n/a**	Speed: **45km/h (28mph)**

MARDER III

SPECIFICATIONS

MARDER III

Type: **four-man tank destroyer**	Effective ceiling: **n/a**
Calibre: **n/a**	Road range: **185km (115 miles)**
Vehicle length: **5.76m (18ft 11in)**	Range: **n/a**
Length of barrel: **n/a**	Projectile weight: **n/a**
Weight travelling: **n/a**	Armour: **14–25mm (.5–1in)**
Weight in action: **10,685kg (23,556lb)**	Engine: **one Praga EPA AC**
Elevation arc: **n/a**	Muzzle velocity: **n/a**
Traverse arc: **n/a**	Speed: **40km/h (25mph)**

Designed as a tank destroyer on the basis of obsolete PzKpfw II Ausf A, C and F light tanks, the 7.5cm PaK 40/2 auf Sfl II (Marder II, or pine marten II) was delivered from 1942. The original tank superstructure and turret were replaced by a boxy open-topped fighting compartment that sloped down to the rear. The PaK 40 gun, complete with its original shield, was mounted on a platform on the front of the vehicle, the gun shield forming a part of the front protective superstructure, and the engine was relocated to the rear. The proximity of the gun shield to the front superstructure limited traverse to 65° and the elevation arc was -5° to +22°, and 37 rounds were carried in total.

With a four-man crew, the Marder II turned the scales at 10,886 kg (23,999 lb). The 7.5cm Pak 40/3 auf Sfl 38 (t) Ausf H (Marder III) was produced during 1942 as a stop-gap tank destroyer, and comprised PaK 40 (with up to 40 rounds) on the chassis of the PzKpfw 38(t) light tank of Czechoslovak origin. The PaK 40's turntable was bolted to the angle section that originally carried the superstructure top plate and the gun shield, up to 15mm (0.59in) thick, was open at the top and rear. The gun could be elevated between -5° and +22°, and traversed 65° left and right. The specifications table at left applies to the Marder III.

STUG III 7.5CM

Otherwise known as the 7.5cm Sturmgeschütz III, the 7.5cm Sturmgeschütz 40 was produced in three SdKfz 142/1 versions as the definitive models of the assault gun series based on the chassis of the PzKpfw III medium tank. The first variants of this four-man vehicle were armed with the 7.5cm KwK L/24 short-barrel gun, and were the StuG III Ausf A that was produced in 1940, the StuG III Ausf B/D with chassis variations, and the StuG III Ausf E of 1942 with an additional armoured pannier on the right-hand side for radio equipment when used as a unit commander's vehicle. The StuG 40 Ausf F that appeared early in 1942 was a development with a cooling fan in the fighting compartment and the more potent 7.5cm Sturmkanone 40 L/43 assault gun development of the KwK 50 tank gun with 54 rounds, while the StuG 40 Ausf F/8 had the longer L/48 version of the same gun. Late in 1942 there appeared the StuG 40 Ausf G, based on the chassis of the PzKpfw III Ausf J tank with the L/48 gun and, in place of the original commander's hatch, a cupola with seven episcopes and an armoured shield for the local-defence machine gun and, on later vehicles, armoured skirts. The final model was the StuG 40 Ausf G (nicknamed the sow's head) with thicker armour and a cast gun mantlet. The data applies to the StuG 40 Ausf F.

SPECIFICATIONS

STUG III 7.5CM

Type: **four-man assault gun**	Effective ceiling: **n/a**
Calibre: **n/a**	Road range: **155km (96 miles)**
Vehicle length: **5.49m (18ft)**	Range: **n/a**
Length of barrel: **n/a**	Projectile weight: **n/a**
Weight travelling: **n/a**	Armour: **30–80mm (1.2–3.15in)**
Weight in action: **21,950kg (24,391lb)**	Engine: **Maybach HL 120 TRM**
Elevation arc: **n/a**	Muzzle velocity: **n/a**
Traverse arc: **n/a**	Speed: **40km/h (25mph)**

FLAK 36/37

SPECIFICATIONS

FLAK 36/37

Type:
towed AA gun

Calibre:
88mm (3.465in)

Vehicle length:
n/a

Length of barrel:
4.93m (1994.1in)

Weight travelling:
6861kg (15,126lb)

Weight in action:
5150kg (11.534lb)

Elevation arc:
-3° to +85°

Traverse arc:
360°

Effective ceiling:
8000m (26,245ft)

Road range:
n/a

Range:
n/a

Projectile weight:
9.24kg (20.34lb)

Armour:
n/a

Engine:
n/a

Muzzle velocity:
820mps (2690fps)

Speed:
n/a

Successor to the pioneering FlaK 18 anti-aircraft gun, which itself remained in first-line service to 1945, the 8.8cm Fliegerabwehrkanone 36 entered service in 1936 as a development of the FlaK 18 with a barrel of different construction and a new carriage. The Rheinmetall-designed barrel had three removable liners, which could be changed when worn and thus removed the need for the replacement of the complete barrel, and the new Sonder Anhänger 202 carriage had double wheels and was towed with the gun aligned to the rear. In 1939 there appeared FlaK 37 development with a revised data-transmission system optimized for the anti-aircraft role so, unlike the dual-role FlaK 18 and 36 anti-tank and anti-aircraft guns, the FlaK 37 was a single-role gun.

The three guns shared a number of components, so it was not uncommon to find the FlaK 18 barrel on the FlaK 37's carriage. The importance of the series is attested by the fact that in August 1944 there were 10,930 examples of the three weapons in service. Examples of the type were also operated by the Italians as the Cannone da 88/56 CA, and self-propelled mountings were the 8.8cm FlaK 37 (Sf) auf Zugkraftwagen 18t and the 8.8cm FlaK 37 auf Sonderfahrgestell. They were excellent weapons.

PAK 43

The 8.8cm Panzerabwehrkanone 43 was a Krupp development of the proposed PaK 42. Entering service late in 1943, this equipment proved itself to be the best anti-tank gun of World War II. The weapon possessed a low silhouette and was also protected by a well-sloped shield, and its potency was revealed by the fact that the PaK 43 was the only German weapon able to penetrate the thick and well-sloped armour of the Soviet IS heavy tanks, and then at ranges well in excess of those offered by smaller-calibre guns. The PaK 43 was odd for a German weapon in using a semi-automatic breech block of the vertically falling type and having electrical firing, and was installed on a cruciform carriage based on that of the 8.8cm FlaK guns: thus the equipment was moved on four wheels with the outrigger arms folded. The PaK 43 could be fired from this wheeled carriage, but the general practice was for the gun to be dug in. Self-propelled mountings for this exceptional weapon were the 8.8cm PaK 43/3 auf Panzerjäger 38(t), the 8.8cm Panzerjäger 43 auf Sfl 38(d), the 8.8cm Pak 43/3 auf Krupp Steyr Sfl 38(d), the Panzerjäger III/IV Nashorn früher Hornisse, the Jagdpanzer Tiger (P) Elefant mit 8.8cm PaK 43/2, the 8.8cm PaK 43/3 auf Panzerjäger Panther, the Jagdpanther (SdKfz 173), and the Jagdtiger für 8.8cm PaK 43 (SdKfz 186).

SPECIFICATIONS

PAK 43

Type: **heavy towed AT gun**	Effective ceiling: **n/a**
Calibre: **88mm (3.46in)**	Road range: **n/a**
Vehicle length: **n/a**	Range: **450m (490 yards)**
Length of barrel: **6.61m (260.25in)**	Projectile weight: **7.3kg (16lb 1.5oz)**
Weight travelling: **5000kg (11,023lb)**	Armour: **n/a**
Weight in action: **n/a**	Engine: **n/a**
Elevation arc: **-8° to +40°**	Muzzle velocity: **1130mps (3707fps)**
Traverse arc: **360°**	Speed: **n/a**

NASHORN

SPECIFICATIONS

NASHORN

Type:
heavy tank destroyer

Effective ceiling:
n/a

Calibre:
n/a

Road range:
185km (115 miles)

Vehicle length:
5.89m (19ft 4in)

Range:
n/a

Length of barrel:
n/a

Projectile weight:
n/a

Weight travelling:
n/a

Armour:
10–30mm (.3–1.18in)

Weight in action:
24,192kg (53,333lb)

Engine:
Maybach HK 120 TRM

Elevation arc:
n/a

Muzzle velocity:
n/a

Traverse arc:
n/a

Speed:
40km/h (25mph)

The five-man vehicle originally called the Hornisse (hornet) but later the Nashorn (rhinoceros) was developed as a tank destroyer armed with the 8.8cm PaK 43 gun, and reached operational service during November 1942. At this time the German Army was heading for defeat at Stalingrad, and the Wehrmacht desperately needed self-propelled anti-tank vehicles to combat the increasing quantities of Red Army tanks on the Eastern Front.

The vehicle comprised the Pak 43/1 gun on the chassis of the PzKpfw IV medium tank with its engine (with the transmission and drive of the PzKpfw III) moved forward to the centre of the hull to provide a clear area for a fighting compartment at the rear. The gun was located over the engine inside a comparatively tall open-topped superstructure of armour 30mm (1.18in) thick at the front and 20mm (0.79in) thick at the sides. Supplied with a maximum of 48 rounds of ammunition, whose shot could penetrate 169mm (6.65in) of armour at 900m (985 yards), the gun could be elevated between -5° and +20°, and traversed 15° left and 15° right of the centreline. When the vehicle was travelling, the gun's long barrel was supported by a lock whose two arms were hinged to the front of the vehicle and looked like an inverted V when clamped the barrel.

JAGDPANTHER

Germany's first efforts to create a decisive tank destroyer by installing the magnificent PaK 43 gun on existing tracked chassis had produced useful but not exceptional vehicles: the PzJäg Tiger (P) "Elefant früher Ferdinand" was too heavy and lacked a machine gun for all-round defence (which proved disastrous at the Battle of Kursk in July 1943, when large numbers were knocked out by Soviet infantry), while the "Hornisse früher Nashorn" was too small and lacked adequate performance.

The obvious solution was use of the PzKpfw V Panther's chassis without a turret but with the armour plate of the front and upper sides extended upwards and roofed over to create well-sloped and enclosed fighting compartment. The 8.8cm Pak 43/3 L/71 gun was located in an aperture in the front plate with protection provided by a heavy cast-steel mantlet inside a cast-steel ring welded to the front plate. Provided with a maximum of 50 rounds of ammunition, the gun could be elevated between -8° and +14°, and traversed 13° left and 13° right of the centreline. Manufacture of the five-man "Jagdpanther" (hunting panther) started during the early part of 1944 on the basis of the Panther Ausf G chassis, and while the first such equipments had a one-piece barrel, the definitive variant had a two-piece barrel.

SPECIFICATIONS

JAGDPANTHER

Type: **heavy tank destroyer**	*Effective ceiling:* **n/a**
Calibre: **n/a**	*Road range:* **200km (124 miles)**
Vehicle length: **9.85m (32ft 4in)**	*Range:* **n/a**
Length of barrel: **n/a**	*Projectile weight:* **n/a**
Weight travelling: **n/a**	*Armour:* **15–80mm (.5–3.15in)**
Weight in action: **45,158kg (99,555lb)**	*Engine:* **Maybach HL 230 P 30**
Elevation arc: **n/a**	*Muzzle velocity:* **n/a**
Traverse arc: **n/a**	*Speed:* **29km/h (18mph)**

FLAK 38/39

SPECIFICATIONS

FLAK 38/39

Type:
heavy towed AA gun

Effective ceiling:
12,800m (41,995ft)

Calibre:
105mm (4.1in)

Road range:
n/a

Vehicle length:
n/a

Range:
n/a

Length of barrel:
6.648m (261.7in)

Projectile weight:
15.1kg (33.3lb)

Weight travelling:
14,600kg (32,187lb)

Armour:
n/a

Weight in action:
10,240kg (22,575lb)

Engine:
n/a

Elevation arc:
-3° to 85°

Muzzle velocity:
880mps (2887fps)

Traverse arc:
360°

Speed:
n/a

Although the German air force's 8.8cm anti-aircraft guns were to prove highly capable weapons, both against aircraft and against armoured vehicles, it became clear in the early 1930s that larger-calibre weapons with a higher muzzle velocity would be needed for the engagement of the high-flying aircraft that were becoming feasible.

In 1933 Krupp and Rheinmetall were each tasked with the construction of a pair of prototypes for competitive evaluation in 1935. Rheinmetall's Gerät 38 was selected in 1936 and ordered as the 10.5cm Fliegerabwehrkanone 38. In basic concept this was an enlarged 8.8cm FlaK 18 with significant changes including the electrical control system and the loading mechanism subsequently adopted for the 8.8cm Flak 41, and the original FlaK 18/36 data-transmission system was replaced with that of the FlaK 37 during 1939, when a sectioned barrel was introduced to create the FlaK 39. The FlaK 38 and 39 were manufactured in quantity, even though they were excelled in performance by the smaller 8.8cm FlaK 41. The gun was generally operated by a commander and nine men, which increased to 11 when manual loading was required. The "88" was an altogether superb weapon which was not rivalled by anything the Allies produced.

LE FH 18

The 10.5cm le FH 18 was designed and developed by Rheinmetall from 1928 and entered service in 1935 as what became the standard medium field howitzer of the German Army up to 1945. The le FH 18 was a completely orthodox but capable and reliable weapon given a somewhat obsolescent look as a result of its large wheels. The type was latter adapted as the le FH 18.M with a muzzle brake to reduce the recoil forces, and could fire a wide variety of shells including high explosive, smoke, tracer, hollow-charge and incendiary. In the period before 1938 the type was exported to Hungary and Spain, and during World War II was installed in a large number of self-propelled mountings.

The one major problem with the le FH 18 was its considerable weight, and in March 1942 there appeared a requirement for a lighter howitzer offering the same capabilities. This led to the le FH 18/40, a weapon that combined the barrel of the le FH 18.M and a modified 7.5cm PaK 40 carriage on which the original wheels were later replaced by larger wheels carrying tyres of greater width. The le FH 18/40 (specification at right) supplemented rather than supplanted the le FH 18. The latter, though, served on all fronts in World War II and gave sterling service to the German Army, proving very reliable in adverse weather conditions.

SPECIFICATIONS

LE FH 18/40

Type:
medium field howitzer

Calibre:
105mm (4.13in)

Vehicle length:
n/a

Length of barrel:
2.71m (106.7in)

Weight travelling:
1955kg (4310lb)

Weight in action:
n/a

Elevation arc:
-6° to +40°

Traverse arc:
56°

Effective ceiling:
n/a

Road range:
n/a

Range:
12,325m (13,480 yards)

Projectile weight:
14.81kg (32.65lb)

Armour:
n/a

Engine:
n/a

Muzzle velocity:
540mps (1772fps)

Speed:
n/a

WESPE

SPECIFICATIONS

WESPE

Type: self-propelled howitzer		**Effective ceiling:** n/a
Calibre: n/a		**Road range:** 145km (90 miles)
Vehicle length: 4.79m (15ft 8.5in)		**Range:** n/a
Length of barrel: n/a		**Projectile weight:** n/a
Weight travelling: n/a		**Armour:** 5–20mm (.2–.79in)
Weight in action: 11,685kg (25,760lb)		**Engine:** one Maybach HL 62 TR
Elevation arc: n/a		**Muzzle velocity:** n/a
Traverse arc: n/a		**Speed:** 39km/h (24.5mph)

Otherwise known as the 10.5cm leichte Feldhaubitze auf Fgst PzKpfw II (Sd) "Wespe" (wasp), the SdKfz 124 was one of Germany's first generation of medium and heavy self-propelled artillery. Such equipment was introduced to service in the middle of 1942 to improve the fighting capability of panzer and motorized infantry divisions, and were hybrid weapons combining existing artillery barrels with the chassis of captured or obsolescent German tanks. As a stopgap measure they worked perfectly well, and were a means of utilizing obsolete tank chassis.

The five-man Wespe was created for the artillery regiments of the panzer divisions, and was in essence the chassis of the PzKpfw II Ausf F light tank with its turret replaced by a fighting compartment, open at the top and the rear, built up from the existing superstructure with armour plate. In the front of this fighting compartment was an aperture for the barrel of the 10.5cm le FH 18/2 howitzer, for which 32 rounds were carried. The le FH 18/2 could be elevated between -5° and +42°, and traversed 17° left and right of the centreline. One the right-hand corner of the superstructure's front there was also a mounting for one 7.92mm MG 34 machine gun (with 600 rounds) for the local defence of the Wespe (weapon on the right in the photograph).

STUG III 10.5CM

Introduced to service in August 1942 and otherwise known as the Sturmhaubitze 42 Ausf F, the five-man 10.5cm Feldhaubitze 42 was basically identical to the Sturmgeschütz 40 Ausf F (SdKfz 142/1) in all major essentials except its armament, which was the powerful 10.5cm Sturmhaubitze 42, an L/18 weapon based on the 10.5cm leichte Feldhaubitze 18. This was installed in an armoured mounting in the front of the raised superstructure of welded steel armour that replaced the turret (as above).

This main armament was provided with 36 rounds of ammunition, though none of this was of the armour-piercing type as the StuH 42 was intended solely for the assault role in support of infantry, but there was no machine gun to provide a local defence capability. The StuH 42 howitzer could be elevated in an arc between -6° and +17°, and the weapon could be traversed 20° left and right of the centreline. The first vehicles had a version of the StuH 42 with a muzzle brake, but later machines were equipped with a howitzer not fitted with a muzzle brake and incapable of firing supercharge ammunition. Smoke dischargers were fitted at the front of the superstructure's sides, and the commander was provided with a cupola with episcopes for all-round vision on the battlefield.

SPECIFICATIONS

STUG III 10.5CM

Type: **SP assault howitzer**	Effective ceiling: **n/a**
Calibre: **n/a**	Road range: **155km (96 miles)**
Vehicle length: **5.50m (18ft 0.5in)**	Range: **n/a**
Length of barrel: **n/a**	Projectile weight: **n/a**
Weight travelling: **n/a**	Armour: **80mm (3.15in)**
Weight in action: **23,370kg (51,520lb)**	Engine: **one Maybach HL 120**
Elevation arc: **n/a**	Muzzle velocity: **n/a**
Traverse arc: **n/a**	Speed: **40km/h (25mph)**

JAGDTIGER

SPECIFICATIONS

JAGDTIGER

Type: **heavy tank destroyer**	Effective ceiling: **n/a**
Calibre: **n/a**	Road range: **160km (99 miles)**
Vehicle length: **10.65m (34ft 11.5in)**	Range: **n/a**
Length of barrel: **n/a**	Projectile weight: **n/a**
Weight travelling: **70,560kg (155,556lb)**	Armour: **30–250mm (1.1–9.95in)**
Weight in action: **n/a**	Engine: **Maybach HL 230 P30**
Elevation arc: **n/a**	Muzzle velocity: **n/a**
Traverse arc: **n/a**	Speed: **38km/h (23.5mph)**

Introduced to service during February 1944 and otherwise known as the Panzerjäger Tiger Ausf B für 12.8cm PaK 44, the six-man Jagdtiger (hunting tiger) was the last word in the German Army's search for a tank hunter/destroyer capable of destroying with a single hit any tank fielded or likely to be fielded by the Allied powers. The Jagdtiger was based on the chassis of the standard Tiger Ausf B (Royal Tiger) with a lengthened suspension and the turret replaced by a massive welded superstructure constituting a virtually impenetrable barbette or fighting compartment. The front of the superstructure was a single piece of cast-steel armour 250mm (9.84in) in thickness and sloped back only 15° from the vertical, and in the centre of this front plate was the 12.8cm PaK 44 gun with a massive cast mantlet to protect the aperture in the front plate.

The side plates were interlocked with the front and rear plates, and entry to the barbette was effected by means of a hatch with double doors. Provided with 38 anti-tank rounds of the separate-loading type, the gun was electrically fired and had a breech block of the vertical sliding type. This gun had an elevation arc between -7.5° to +15°, and could be traversed 10° left and right of the centreline. However, there were never enough to make a difference on the battlefield.

KANONE 44

When they invaded the USSR in June 1941, the Germans made rapid and very extensive gains against Soviet forces that were poorly trained, badly led and often equipped with obsolescent if not obsolete weapons. One exception, though, was Soviet medium artillery which, as the Germans rapidly found, was technically excellent in many respects. In an effort to provide the German Army with improved weapons in the 128mm calibre, Krupp created the 12.8cm Kanone 43 as a structurally light gun with a screw breech rather than the usual sliding block, but this found no favour, for better 12.8cm K 44 (sometimes 12.8cm PaK 44) weapons were offered by Rheinmetall-Borsig as well as Krupp as field guns with a potent anti-tank capability on a carriage offering 360° traverse. The two guns were generally similar in performance, but the Krupp weapon was preferred as its four-wheel carriage offered production advantages over the more complicated six-wheel carriage of the Rheinmetall weapon. Production of the K 44 never rose above a trickle as a result of production problems, however, and at the end of World War II the German Army had received only a few of these impressive weapons. A version of the K 44 for installation in armoured vehicles was the 12.8cm KwK 82, which was installed in the Jagdtiger tank destroyer.

SPECIFICATIONS

KANONE 44

Type: **heavy towed field gun**	Effective ceiling: **n/a**
Calibre: **128mm (5.04in)**	Road range: **n/a**
Vehicle length: **n/a**	Range: **24,400m (26,685 yards)**
Length of barrel: **6.625m (260.8in)**	Projectile weight: **28.3kg (62.4lb)**
Weight travelling: **unknown**	Armour: **n/a**
Weight in action: **10,160kg (22,39lb)**	Engine: **n/a**
Elevation arc: **-7° to +45° 27'**	Muzzle velocity: **920mps (3018fps)**
Traverse arc: **360°**	Speed: **n/a**

S IG 33

SPECIFICATIONS

S IG 33

Type:
infantry support gun

Calibre:
149.1mm (5.87in)

Vehicle length:
n/a

Length of barrel:
1.650m (64.9in)

Weight travelling:
unknown

Weight in action:
1750kg (3858lb)

Elevation arc:
0° to +73°

Traverse arc:
11° 30'

Effective ceiling:
n/a

Road range:
n/a

Range:
4700m (5140 yards)

Projectile weight:
38kg (83.8lb)

Armour:
n/a

Engine:
n/a

Muzzle velocity:
240mps (787fps)

Speed:
n/a

Of all the German infantry support guns produced for service in World War II, the most capable and powerful was the 15cm schwere Infanteriegeschütz 33. Produced by the Rheinmetall-Borsig company from 1927, the s IG 33 was a large item of equipment that gave the impression, largely as a result of its steel wheels with a diameter of 1.10m (43.3in), of being somewhat old fashioned. In this instance appearance was deceptive, for the s IG 33 was capable and very reliable, and as a result the weapon remained in large-scale service right up to the end of World War II in 1945. The s IG 33 had good minimum and maximum range capabilities for a weapon of its type, and could fire virtually the full range of ammunition types (including the 89.5kg/197.3lb muzzle-launched stick bomb to "take out" strongpoints and barbed wire entanglements out to a range of 1025m/1120 yards) for a weapon of its type. The s IG 33's main drawback was its high weight, and before the outbreak of war in 1939 the Germans developed a carriage of light alloy rather than steel manufacture, which was then not put into production. So it was only after self-propelled mountings had been developed that the s IG 33 (later developed into the Sturmhaubitze 43 L/12 weapon) really came into its own. These mountings included the 15cm s IG 33 auf GW I Ausf B.

KANONE 39

In the 1930s Krupp responded to a requirement of the Turkish Army with the development of a powerful gun in 150mm calibre. Production got under way in the later stages of the decade, but delivery of the first completed weapons was prevented by the outbreak of World War II in September 1939 (notwithstanding its spectacular victories, the German Army entered the war with a shortage of equipment). In 1940, therefore, the German Army decided to adopt the weapons for dual-role service in the heavy field and coastal-defence roles. In the former the weapon was fired on its split-trail carriage, while long-range accuracy in the latter role was enhanced when the weapon was fired from a mobile turntable carried by a special transport: when the gun was operated in this task, after the turntable had been dug in, the trails were connected as a single unit and the whole equipment could be traversed through 360° by operation of a mechanism powered by the rotation of a handle. For road movement the K 39 was moved in three loads (barrel and transporter, carriage, and platform and transporter). The K 39 was a capable piece of artillery and remained in production until the end of the war in 1945. The main problem with large-calibre artillery pieces was the general lack of prime movers to move them to and from the battlefield.

SPECIFICATIONS

KANONE 39

Type: **heavy towed field gun**	Effective ceiling: **n/a**
Calibre: **149.1mm (5.87in)**	Road range: **n/a**
Vehicle length: **n/a**	Range: **24,700m (27,010 yards)**
Length of barrel: **7.868mm (309.7in)**	Projectile weight: **43kg (94.8lb)**
Weight travelling: **n/a**	Armour: **n/a**
Weight in action: **12,200kg (26,896lb)**	Engine: **n/a**
Elevation arc: **-3 to +46°**	Muzzle velocity: **865mps (2838fps)**
Traverse arc: **60–360°**	Speed: **n/a**

HUMMEL

SPECIFICATIONS

HUMMEL

Type:
SP heavy howitzer

Effective ceiling:
n/a

Calibre:
n/a

Road range:
200km (124 miles)

Vehicle length:
6.67m (21ft 11in)

Range:
n/a

Length of barrel:
n/a

Projectile weight:
n/a

Weight travelling:
n/a

Armour:
10–30mm (.3–1.18in)

Weight in action:
23,500kg (51,808lb)

Engine:
Maybach HL 120 TRM

Elevation arc:
n/a

Muzzle velocity:
n/a

Traverse arc:
n/a

Speed:
42km/h (26mph)

Otherwise known as the 15cm schwere Panzerhaubitze 18/1 (Sf) auf Fgst PzKpfw III/IV or as the Geschützwagen III/IV, the five-man "Hummel" (bumble bee) was produced from 1942 for service from the autumn of 1943 as an item of self-propelled heavy field artillery. Such artillery entered German Army service only in 1942, and was intended to provide artillery support for panzer and motorized infantry divisions. Various obsolescent German tank chassis were employed, together with those of captured French tanks, and the Hummel was based on a hybrid chassis based on that of the suspension and track work of the PzKpfw IV with the engine, transmission and final drive of the PzKpfw III. The engine was relocated to the centre of the tank, allowing the construction over the rear of the vehicle of a comparatively high and open-topped fighting compartment of well-sloped but light armour. The 15cm schwere Feldhaubitze 18/1 was installed with its barrel projecting through an aperture in the front of the fighting compartment, and was provided with only 18 rounds of ammunition. The gun could be elevated through an arc between -3° and +40°, and traversed a mere 3° left and right of the centreline. A 7.92mm MG 34 or MG 42 machine gun was provided for local defence.

BRUMMBÄR

Otherwise known as the Sturmpanzer 43 or 15 cm Sturmhaubitze 43 L/12 auf Fgst PzKpfw IV (Sd), the five-man Sturmpanzer IV Brummbär (grizzly bear) was created to meet the needs of the German Army on the Eastern Front for a heavy assault gun carrying a 149.1mm howitzer, the Sturmhaubitze 42 weapon that had only an L/12 barrel and was developed from the schwere Infanteriegeschütz 33. This was fitted in a ball mounting that extended from the 100mm (3.94in) thick front of the fixed superstructure via a large mantlet and sleeve of cast armour.

The superstructure was of thick plate and built up over the hull of a PzKpfw IV Ausf F, G, H or J medium tank. This mounting gave the howitzer an elevation arc between -8 and +30°, and a traverse arc of 20° left and right of the centreline. The howitzer was provided with 38 rounds of ammunition that could fire a 38kg (83.8lb) projectile to a range of 4275m (4675yards) with a muzzle velocity of 240m (787ft) per second. Production of the Brummbär totalled only 313 vehicles. Like many innovative German designs that entered production towards the end of the war, there were never enough to tip the scales in Germany's favour. Though they could achieve local victories, they were a case of too little, far too late.

SPECIFICATIONS

BRUMMBÄR

Type:
SP assault howitzer

Calibre:
n/a

Vehicle length:
5.91m (19ft 5in)

Length of barrel:
n/a

Weight travelling:
n/a

Weight in action:
28,650kg (63,161lb)

Elevation arc:
n/a

Traverse arc:
n/a

Effective ceiling:
n/a

Road range:
200km (124 miles)

Range:
n/a

Projectile weight:
n/a

Armour:
20–100mm (.8–3.94in)

Engine:
Maybach HL 120 TRM

Muzzle velocity:
n/a

Speed:
40km/h (25mph)

QF 2-PDR

SPECIFICATIONS

QF 2-PDR

Type:
light towed AT gun

Effective ceiling:
n/a

Calibre:
40mm (1.575in)

Road range:
n/a

Vehicle length:
n/a

Range:
655m (600 yards)

Length of barrel:
2.08m (81.95in)

Projectile weight:
1.07kg (2lb 6oz)

Weight travelling:
832kg (1848lb)

Armour:
n/a

Weight in action:
n/a

Engine:
n/a

Elevation arc:
-13° to +15°

Muzzle velocity:
792mps (2616fps)

Traverse arc:
360°

Speed:
n/a

Work on the design and development of the 2-pdr anti-tank gun began in 1934, and the weapon entered service in 1938 as a solidly constructed but decidedly heavy equipment that was more than twice the weight of its German counterpart, the 3.7cm Pak 35/36. This resulted from the fact that the gun was planned as a defensive weapon firing from concealment, and was therefore installed on a carriage offering 360° traverse and mounted on a tripod platform. In fact, many British artillery pieces were heavier than their German equivalents, which inhibited mobility on the battlefield.

In 1940 the gun proved successful in the French campaign, though considering that the majority of German tanks were light PzKpfw I and II models, this is hardly surprising. Large numbers were abandoned in the Dunkirk evacuation and seized by the Germans for service as 4cm PaK 192(e) coastal-defence weapons. The gun was already obsolete but maintained in production for lack of any replacement, and from mid-1942 was withdrawn from service with Royal Artillery anti-tank batteries for infantry use. The gun was used in the Far East, against the more lightly protected Japanese tanks, to 1945. The 2-pdr gun was manufactured by Vickers-Armstrongs in several marks that differed in detail, and the usual carriage was the Carriage 2-pdr Mark III.

QF 6-PDR

The need for a towed anti-tank gun of larger calibre became evident even as the 2-pdr was entering service in 1938, and the 6-pdr first guns were delivered in September 1941. The Mk I first gun was not retained in service and was replaced by the short-barrel Mk II that was then replaced by the longer-barrel Mk IV (the Mks III and V were tank guns).

Within a year the 6-pdr needed a successor as it could not tackle the frontal armour of the PzKpfw VI Tiger heavy tank, and from 1943 it was succeeded in the Royal Artillery's anti-tank batteries by the 17-pdr and relegated to infantry use, in which it lasted to the end of World War II. Some were passed over to the Soviets and the Americans built a copy as the 57mm Anti-tank Gun M1. There were few carriage modifications as the Carriages 6-pdr 7 cwt Mks I, IA, and II differed only in detail, and the Mk III intended for use by airborne divisions was thus lighter. Self-propelled mountings were the Carrier, AEC, 6-pdr Gun, Mk I (Deacon), the Morris Mk II (Firefly) and the SP 6-pdr Gun Alecto Mk II. The 6-pdr was capable of penetrating 69mm (2.7in) of armour at a range of 915m (1000 yards). This performance was satisfactory against light and medium enemy tanks, but was woefully inadequate against such vehicles as the Tiger, which had armour at least 100mm (4in) thick.

SPECIFICATIONS

QF 6-PDR

Type: **medium towed AT gun**	Effective ceiling: **n/a**
Calibre: **57mm (2.244in)**	Road range: **n/a**
Vehicle length: **n/a**	Range: **unknown**
Length of barrel: **2.44m (101in)**	Projectile weight: **2.84kg (6.2lb)**
Weight travelling: **1112kg (2471lb)**	Armour: **n/a**
Weight in action: **n/a**	Engine: **n/a**
Elevation arc: **-5° to +15°**	Muzzle velocity: **823mps (2700fps)**
Traverse arc: **90°**	Speed: **n/a**

QF 3IN AA

SPECIFICATIONS

QF 3IN AA

Type: **medium towed AA gun**	Effective ceiling: **7165m (23,500ft)**
Calibre: **76.2mm (3in)**	Road range: **n/a**
Vehicle length: **n/a**	Range: **n/a**
Length of barrel: **3.42m (134.8in)**	Projectile weight: **7.26kg (16lb)**
Weight travelling: **977kg (17,585lb)**	Armour: **n/a**
Weight in action: **unknown**	Engine: **n/a**
Elevation arc: **-10° to +90°**	Muzzle velocity: **610mps (2000fps)**
Traverse arc: **360°**	Speed: **n/a**

The 3in 20 cwt anti-aircraft gun was a long-lived type that entered service in 1914 and disappeared from service only in 1946. In this 33-year period the type was steadily improved, with the result that on the outbreak of World War II in 1939 the gun was still moderately effective, especially against Luftwaffe medium bombers. The pace of the improvement programme meant that in September 1939 there were eight marks of gun in service, some of them with a sliding breech block arrangement and others with an interrupted-screw breech block arrangement, but by the same date most of the guns had barrels with loose liners. The mountings on which the guns were installed were also very varied: some were located statically on concrete or steel beds, while others were installed on two- or four-wheeled (three marks) carriages, and others still were embarked on lorries.

Many anti-aircraft gunners preferred the 3in gun to its planned successor, the 3.7in gun, as the older weapon was easier to move and handle. Many examples of the former were also employed for training, and guns seized by the Germans in 1940 were used with the revised designation 7.5cm Flak Vickers(e). The gun saw service in most theatres of the war, proving a reliable weapon in varying climatic conditions.

ARCHER

The four-man Archer self-propelled anti-tank gun was based on the chassis of the Valentine infantry tank and was highly unusual in the fact that the 17-pdr anti-tank gun, a 3in weapon provided with 39 rounds, faced to the rear. The idea behind this novel feature was that the vehicle could position itself in order to ambush enemy tanks, then escape with speed once the trap had been sprung.

The gun was originally a towed equipment (large shield, split trail arrangement and two wheels) designed to succeed the 6-pdr, entered service in August 1942, and fired a 7.65kg (17lb) shot at 884m (2900ft) per second to penetrate 130mm (5.12in) of armour at 915m (1000 yards) at 30°. This made the 17-pdr one of the finest anti-tank guns of World War II. Possessing an elevation arc between -7° and +15° and a traverse arc of 45°, the Archer's gun was installed in an armoured super-structure at the extreme front of the vehicle. This superstructure was usually open-topped, but later production vehicles had a light steel roof. An order for 800 such vehicles was placed with Vickers-Armstrongs (Elswick), and the vehicles entered service early in 1944, and production was terminated at the end of hostilities in 1945 after the completion of 665 vehicles that served with anti-tank regiments in northwestern Europe and Italy.

SPECIFICATIONS

ARCHER

Type: **self-propelled AT gun**	Effective ceiling: **n/a**
Calibre: **n/a**	Road range: **145km (90 miles)**
Vehicle length: **6.68m (21ft 11in)**	Range: **n/a**
Length of barrel: **n/a**	Projectile weight: **n/a**
Weight travelling: **n/a**	Armour: **8–60mm (.3–2.36in)**
Weight in action: **16,257kg (35,840lb)**	Engine: **one GMC diesel**
Elevation arc: **n/a**	Muzzle velocity: **n/a**
Traverse arc: **n/a**	Speed: **24km/h (15mph)**

QF 25-PDR

SPECIFICATIONS

QF 25-PDR

Type: medium gun/howitzer	**Effective ceiling:** n/a
Calibre: 87.6mm (3.45in)	**Road range:** n/a
Vehicle length: n/a	**Range:** 12,255m (13,400 yards)
Length of barrel: 2.35m (92.5in)	**Projectile weight:** 11.34kg (25lb)
Weight travelling: 1801kg (3968lb)	**Armour:** n/a
Weight in action: n/a	**Engine:** n/a
Elevation arc: -5° to +40°	**Muzzle velocity:** 532mps (1745fps)
Traverse arc: 8°– 360°	**Speed:** n/a

During 1936 the Royal Artillery issued a requirement for an improved gun/howitzer providing a range of 12,345m (13,500 yards) or more. This was beyond the capability of the current 18/25-pdr Mk I conversion from 18-pdr standard, so the 25-pdr Mk II was designed, one of the most famous artillery pieces of World War II. This was at first to have possessed a split-trail carriage, but finally appeared with a humped box trail combined with a 360° firing platform.

The new equipment entered service in mid-1940, and by 1945 more than 12,000 had been completed. Strong, reliable and handy, the 25-pdr served in every British and Commonwealth theatre, and in North Africa doubled as an anti-tank gun (until the advent of the 17-pdr) with a telescopic sight and double-baffle muzzle brake. The 25-pdr gun remained essentially unaltered throughout its production life, but a narrower Mk II carriage was developed for jungle and airborne service, while the Mk III carriage had a hinged trail for increased elevation capability in mountainous regions. The Germans equipped several artillery regiments with captured 25-pdr guns, which they designated as the 8.76cm Feldkanone 280(e). British self-propelled mountings included the Carrier, Valentine, 25-pdr Gun, Mk I, Bishop and the 25-pdr, SP, Tracked, Sexton.

QF 3.7IN AA

In 1933, after a delay dating from 1920, the British finally issued a requirement for a 3.7in anti-aircraft gun, and Vickers-Armstrongs completed a prototype during 1936. The new gun entered service in 1938, but deliveries were slow because the manufacture of the complex carriage was considerably slower than that of the straightforward gun. The gun was produced in three marks and was of modern design with a loose liner, and though the four-wheel mounting was intended to make the weapon fully mobile, its weight meant that the equipment could be classified only as semi-mobile.

With gun manufacture outstripping construction of the Mks I, IA, III and IIIA mobile mountings, other companies were called into the programme to produce the less complicated Mks II and IIA/C fixed mountings for the protection of high-priority targets. The design was later simplified to ease manufacture, power rammers and automatic fuse setters were added, and predictors and data-transmission systems were upgraded to make the 3.7in gun more reliable and more capable. The Germans used captured examples with the designation 9.4cm FlaK Vickers M.39(e), for which they manufactured 100,000 rounds of ammunition early in 1943. The data in the specifications box refers to the Mk III gun on Mk III mounting.

SPECIFICATIONS

QF 3.7IN AA

Type: **heavy towed AA gun**	Effective ceiling: **9755m (32,000ft)**
Calibre: **94mm (3.7in)**	Road range: **n/a**
Vehicle length: **n/a**	Range: **n/a**
Length of barrel: **4.7m (185in)**	Projectile weight: **12.96kg (28.56lb)**
Weight travelling: **9317kg (20,540lb)**	Armour: **n/a**
Weight in action: **unknown**	Engine: **n/a**
Elevation arc: **-5° to +80°**	Muzzle velocity: **793mps (2600fps)**
Traverse arc: **360°**	Speed: **n/a**

4.5IN GUN MK II

SPECIFICATIONS

4.5IN GUN MK II

Type: **heavy towed gun**	Effective ceiling: **n/a**
Calibre: **114.3mm (4.5in)**	Road range: **n/a**
Vehicle length: **n/a**	Range: **18,745m (20,500 yards)**
Length of barrel: **4.764m (187.55in)**	Projectile weight: **24.97kg (55lb)**
Weight travelling: **15,251kg (33,600lb)**	Armour: **n/a**
Weight in action: **5842kg (12,880lb)**	Engine: **n/a**
Elevation arc: **-5° to 45°**	Muzzle velocity: **686mps (2250fps)**
Traverse arc: **60°**	Speed: **n/a**

In the later part of the 1930s, when it was appreciated that the current programme of adapting existing 60-pdr gun carriages to take a new 4.5in gun barrel would not satisfy the full requirement of the Royal Artillery's medium regiments, the British Army decided to create a new equipment that combined a new 4.5in gun on the carriage being planned for the new 5.5in howitzer.

The design and development of the new gun was complete by 1940, but the programme was then checked by problems with the new carriage. In fact, the design was developed and built by 1940, but difficulties with the new carriage meant that it was 1941 before the equipment entered service. The task of the 4.5in gun was long-range interdiction and counter-battery fire, but experience soon revealed that capability in these tasks was hampered by the modest 1.76kg (3.875lb) high explosive load of the shell. Production priority was then switched to the 5.5in howitzer, and the last 4.5in guns were pulled out of service after the end of World War II in 1945. The gun was conventional in concept and average in performance but notable for its strength, while the two carriage variants, which differed only in modest detail, were of the split-trail type and featured very prominent equilibrators. It served the British Army well in its various campaigns.

5.5IN GUN MK III

It was in the middle of the 1930s that the British Army decided that the Royal Artillery required a thoroughly modern long-range gun for the counter-battery and interdiction roles. The result was to exceed all expectations, and would create a gun that was to have a career of some 40 years.

A requirement was accordingly issued for a 5in (127mm) gun to fire a 45.4kg (100lb) shell over a range of 14,630 m (16,000 yards). The requirement was altered in 1939 to cover a gun of 140mm (5.5in) calibre, and prototype guns were successfully evaluated in 1940. Designed for the originally schemed 5in weapon, the carriage was too light for the larger-calibre weapon, so a new carriage had to be created and the new equipment thus entered service only in 1941. From this time onward, however, the 5.5in guns proved to be a major success, and the type remained in service with some armies into the early 1980s.

Firing a heavier shell (with a proportionally greater high explosive load for greater destructive effect) to a slightly shorter range, the 5.5in gun was generally superior to the 4.5in gun, and was used as much as a howitzer as a gun. The normal projectile weight was 45.4kg (100lb), though the gun also fired a lighter round that weighed 36.32kg (80lb).

SPECIFICATIONS

5.5IN GUN MK III

Type: **heavy towed gun**	Effective ceiling: **n/a**
Calibre: **139.7mm (5.5in)**	Road range: **n/a**
Vehicle length: **n/a**	Range: **14,815m (16,200 yards)**
Length of barrel: **4.176m (164.4in)**	Projectile weight: **36.32kg (80lb)**
Weight travelling: **n/a**	Armour: **n/a**
Weight in action: **5792kg (12,770lb)**	Engine: **n/a**
Elevation arc: **-5° to +45°**	Muzzle velocity: **762mps (2500fps)**
Traverse arc: **60°**	Speed: **n/a**

6IN GUN MK VII

SPECIFICATIONS

6IN GUN MK VII

Type: **heavy towed gun**	Effective ceiling: **n/a**
Calibre: **152.4mm (6in)**	Road range: **n/a**
Vehicle length: **n/a**	Range: **16,595m (18,150 yards)**
Length of barrel: **5.58m (219.7in)**	Projectile weight: **45.4kg (100lb)**
Weight travelling: **unknown**	Armour: **n/a**
Weight in action: **10,999kg (24,250lb)**	Engine: **n/a**
Elevation arc: **0° to +38°**	Muzzle velocity: **770mps (2525fps)**
Traverse arc: **8°**	Speed: **n/a**

The 6in Gun Mk VIII saw only the most limited and specialized service in the course of World War II. The equipment had been created in World War I as the combination of a 6in gun surplus to naval and coastal defence requirements, on the carriage of the 8in Howitzer Mks VII and VIII.

The weapon saw only limited service with the British, but there were sufficient equipments on hand when the USA entered World War I in April 1917 for that country, which had an acute lack of heavy artillery suitable for service on the Western Front, to buy substantial numbers for service with the revised designation 6in Gun M1917. The surviving equipments were shipped to the Panama Canal Zone after the end of the war and there became coast-defence weapons on special concrete "Panama Mount" firing platforms (similar to those in the above photograph). These weapons were never used in anger against an enemy.

By 1939 the weapons had been fitted with large pneumatic tyres for improved mobility but were nonetheless completely obsolete and on the verge of being scrapped when Brazil bought just under 100 to improve her coastal defences. As the Germans never launched an amphibious invasion of the British Isles, the guns were never called upon to fulfil their duty.

6IN GUN MK XIX

The first pattern of 6in guns for service with the British Army were created for the long-range bombardment role in World War I, and of the very many marks only the 6in Gun Mk XIX survived in first-line service at the beginning of World War II in 1939. World War I had seen a huge rise in heavy artillery strengths due to the demands of trench warfare. Ironically, as the major powers thought that the next war would be similar, large numbers of heavy artillery pieces had been held in reserve. Great Britain was no different, and stockpiled pieces up to 18in in calibre.

The 6in Gun had originally been installed on the carriage of the 8in Howitzer with large-diameter traction engine wheels and a substantial box trail. But modest improvement in the 1930s had included more modern wheels with pneumatic tyres for high-speed traction. When Germany attacked France in May 1940, the British Expeditionary Force had only 13 examples of this obsolescent weapon in its inventory. The Germans seized all of these weapons as they were too heavy for evacuation from Dunkirk (one of the disadvantages of heavy artillery pieces), and then scrapped the weapons for their steel. The few such equipments still in Great Britain were installed at carefully surveyed sites as coast-defence weapons.

SPECIFICATIONS

6IN GUN MK XIX

Type:
heavy towed gun

Calibre:
152.4mm (6in)

Vehicle length:
n/a

Length of barrel:
5.33mm (210in)

Weight travelling:
10338kg (22,790lb)

Weight in action:
unknown

Elevation arc:
0° to +38°

.Traverse arc:
8°

Effective ceiling:
n/a

Road range:
n/a

Range:
17,145m (18,750 yards)

Projectile weight:
about 45.4kg (100lb)

Armour:
n/a

Engine:
n/a

Muzzle velocity:
733mps (2405fps)

Speed:
n/a

6IN HOWITZER MK I

SPECIFICATIONS

6IN HOWITZER MK I

Type: heavy towed howitzer	**Effective ceiling:** n/a
Calibre: 152.4mm (6in)	**Road range:** n/a
Vehicle length: n/a	**Range:** 10,425m (11,400 yards)
Length of barrel: 2.027m (79.8in)	**Projectile weight:** 45.48kg (100.19lb)
Weight travelling: 4468kg (9850lb)	**Armour:** n/a
Weight in action: unknown	**Engine:** n/a
Elevation arc: 0° to +45°	**Muzzle velocity:** 430mps (1410fps)
Traverse arc: 8°	**Speed:** n/a

Work on the design of the weapon that became the 6in 26 cwt Howitzer started in 1915. The weapon entered service later in the same year, and large-scale manufacture meant that by the war's end in 1918 more than 4000 such weapons were in use. Few changes were ever effected in the weapon, and the carriage was updated only in the late 1930s with the adoption of the Mks IP and IR carriages characterized by pneumatic tyres. In 1939 the 6in howitzer was the most numerous item of artillery in the Royal Artillery regiments of the British Expeditionary Force despatched to France after the start of World War II.

Most of these 220 or so weapons were captured by the Germans and later placed in service as 15.2cm schwere Feldhaubitze 412(e) pieces. The weapons left in British hands were used mainly for training, although some saw service during 1941 in North Africa and Eritrea. In the early 1920s weapons of this type had been exported to four other countries, but the Soviet equipments had been phased out of service by 1941 and those of the other three (together with their final German designations) were the Belgian Obusier de 6in (15.2cm schwere Feldhaubitze 410[b]), the Dutch Houwitzer 6in (15.2cm sFH 407[h]) and the Italian Obice da 152/13 (15.2cm sFH 412[i]).

7.2IN HOWITZER MK V

By the mid-1930s the British Army had perceived the need for a whole new range of modern artillery, but lacked the funding for large-scale design, development and production. Thus after its expulsion from mainland Europe in June 1940, when all heavy weapons had to be abandoned as they were too heavy to get to the Channel before the Germans overtook them, the British Army was woefully short of modern equipment (it was a small comfort that the Germans scrapped most of the large pieces and recycled the metal).

Among the many expediencies now forced on the army was the creation of a "new" howitzer: old 8in howitzer barrels were fitted with a new 183mm (7.2in) liner to produce the 7.2in Howitzer. This interim weapon proved very useful and soon there were demands for more such weapons despite the fact that the weapon recoiled so heavily that wooden ramps had to be added behind the wheels to check the recoil, which required the howitzer to be re-laid before being fired once more. Among the several barrel variants were the Mks I, I*, II, III, IV and V that differed only in the type of 8in barrel from which they were created. Entering service in 1941, the 7.2in Howitzer remained in widespread service to 1945. It gave sterling service to the British Army.

SPECIFICATIONS

7.2IN HOWITZER MK V

Type: **heavy towed howitzer**	Effective ceiling: **n/a**
Calibre: **182.9mm (7.2in)**	Road range: **n/a**
Vehicle length: **n/a**	Range: **15,455m (16,900 yards)**
Length of barrel: **4.092m (161.1in)**	Projectile weight: **91.7kg (202lb)**
Weight travelling: **10,387kg (22,900lb)**	Armour: **n/a**
Weight in action: **n/a**	Engine: **n/a**
Elevation arc: **0° to +45°**	Muzzle velocity: **518mps (1700fps)**
Traverse arc: **8°**	Speed: **n/a**

7.2IN HOWITZER MK VI

SPECIFICATIONS

7.2IN HOWITZER MK VI

Type:
heavy towed howitzer

Effective ceiling:
n/a

Calibre:
182.9mm (7.2in)

Road range:
n/a

Vehicle length:
n/a

Range:
17,990m (19,675 yards)

Length of barrel:
6.30m (248in)

Projectile weight:
91.7kg (200lb)

Weight travelling:
n/a

Armour:
n/a

Weight in action:
13,211kg (29,125lb)

Engine:
n/a

Elevation arc:
-2° to +65°

Muzzle velocity:
497mps (1630fps)

Traverse arc:
60°

Speed:
n/a

The 7.2in Howitzer Mks I to V weapons were created in 1940 by relining 8in (203mm) howitzer barrels to create very useful weapons firing an effective shell, but were tactically hampered by their obsolete carriage of the box trail type with large-diameter wheels only marginally improved by the use of pneumatic tyres. In 1944, therefore, a significantly longer L/34.4 barrel was introduced in succession to the original L/23.7 barrel to create the Gun Mk VI, and this was installed on an altogether more modern carriage, namely that common to the American 155mm Gun M1 and 8in Howitzer M1.

This carriage was of the split-trail type with four pairs of pneumatically tyred wheels on two axles. The new carriage provided far better firing stability and thus much improved range without loss of accuracy to create a very useful weapon. The earlier weapons were withdrawn as the new combination became available. It is worth noting that modest numbers of Mks I and I* barrels were also installed on the US carriage to become Mk V* weapons, and repaired examples of the Mk VI gun were known as Mk VI/1 weapons. The gun was used throughout Europe between 1944 and 1945. Massed in batteries it proved very effective in breaching and reducing German defensive positions.

GUN 75/27 MO 11

The general poverty of Italian artillery design capability in the first part of the twentieth century is attested by the fact that the two standard 75mm field guns adopted in the period before World War I's beginning in 1914 were of non-Italian design, for in addition to the German-created modello 06 there was the French-designed Cannone da 75/27 modello 11. This latter offered much the same performance as the modello 06, but in some respects was a more advanced battlefield weapon.

The most impressive features were the use of a split-trail arrangement with the spade plates that were then becoming accepted as a means of improving the equipment's stability as the gun was fired, and a recoil mechanism that remained fixed regardless of the barrel's elevation. The modello 11 was schemed as a cavalry support weapon, but was so successful that it was also issued to batteries of standard field artillery. In June 1940 the Italian Army still had some 1800 75mm guns on strength, and a large proportion of these were modello 11 weapons. Those that survived to 1943 were then seized by the Germans for service with the revised designation 7.5cm Feldkanone 244(i). However, by this stage of the war they were of little use apart from in anti-partisan operations.

SPECIFICATIONS

GUN 75/27 MO 11

Type: **light towed gun**	Effective ceiling: **n/a**
Calibre: **75mm (2.95in)**	Road range: **n/a**
Vehicle length: **n/a**	Range: **10,240m (11,200 yards)**
Length of barrel: **2.132m (83.9in)**	Projectile weight: **6.35kg (14lb)**
Weight travelling: **1900kg (4189lb)**	Armour: **n/a**
Weight in action: **1076kg (2372lb)**	Engine: **n/a**
Elevation arc: **-15° to +65°**	Muzzle velocity: **502mps (1647fps)**
Traverse arc: **52°9'**	Speed: **n/a**

GUN 90/53 SEMOVENTE

SPECIFICATIONS

GUN 90/53 SEMOVENTE

Type: **SP anti-tank**	Effective ceiling: **n/a**
Calibre: **90mm (3.54in)**	Road range: **200km (124 miles)**
Vehicle length: **5.2m (17ft 1in)**	Range: **n/a**
Length of barrel: **n/a**	Projectile weight: **n/a**
Weight travelling: **n/a**	Armour: **10–40mm (.39–1.58in)**
Weight in action: **17,275kg (38,084lb)**	Engine: **SPA 15 TM 41**
Elevation arc: **-2° to +85°**	Muzzle velocity: **n/a**
Traverse arc: **360°**	Speed: **35km/h (21.75mph)**

By 1939, the Italian Army had recognized the need for an anti-aircraft gun of larger calibre than its current 75mm mainstay. Ansaldo completed the first Cannone da 90/53 CA later in the same year. Test firing revealed that this was a good weapon, and it was rapidly ordered into production in three versions.

The four-man Semovente modello 41M da 90/53 self-propelled anti-tank gun was a very effective equipment and comprised the Cannone da 90/53 gun on a modified Carro Armato modello 14/41 tank chassis. The equipment was planned to provide the Italian forces on the Eastern Front with a means to "kill" the Soviet T-34 medium tank, but in the event none was ever sent to this theatre: 24 of the 30 modello 41M vehicles that were eventually completed were used in the Sicilian campaign of July 1943 with Italian crews under German tactical command. The gun was installed over the rear of the vehicle behind a substantial armoured shield offering lateral as well as frontal protection, and the long barrel was supported in the travelling position by a lock over the front of the vehicle. The gun possessed an elevation arc between -5° and +24° as well as a traverse arc of 80°. Six rounds were carried on the vehicle, with another 26 on an accompanying armoured ammunition carrier that towed an trailer with a further 40 rounds.

GUN 149/40 MO 35

Designed to provide the Italian Army with a replacement for its ancient Cannone da 149/35 heavy gun dating from the turn of the 19th century, the prototype of a new 149mm weapon was completed by Ansaldo in 1934 and then ordered into production as the Cannone da 149/40 modello 35 in the following year. By the time of Italy's entry into World War II some 590 such equipments had been ordered but by September 1941 only slightly more than 50 were in first-line service.

The modello 35 had an advanced design that ensured that the weight of the gun was off the wheels when fired, but the large split trails were anchored by hammered trail spikes and, to ensure stability when the gun was fired, the wheels were not removed. There is little doubt that the modello 35 was among the best pieces of artillery used by the Italians in World War II, but the importance of the type was greatly diminished by the small number of equipments completed. For movement the modello 35 was divided into two loads towed by tractors. In 1943 the Germans seized all of the weapons that they could for service with the designation 15cm Kanone 408(i), and Ansaldo produced a further 12 specifically for German service, indicating that the German Army liked the weapon.

SPECIFICATIONS

GUN 149/40 MO 35

Type: **heavy towed gun**	Effective ceiling: **n/a**
Calibre: **149.1mm (5.87in)**	Road range: **n/a**
Vehicle length: **n/a**	Range: **23,700m (25,920 yards)**
Length of barrel: **5.964m (234.8in)**	Projectile weight: **46kg (101.4lb)**
Weight travelling: **n/a**	Armour: **n/a**
Weight in action: **11,340kg (25,000lb)**	Engine: **n/a**
Elevation arc: **0° to +45°**	Muzzle velocity: **800mps (2625fps)**
Traverse arc: **60°**	Speed: **n/a**

GUN 149/19 MO 41

SPECIFICATIONS

GUN 149/19 MO 41

Type: **heavy towed howitzer**	Effective ceiling: **n/a**
Calibre: **149.1mm (5.87 in)**	Road range: **n/a**
Vehicle length: **n/a**	Range: **14,250m (15,585 yards)**
Length of barrel: **2.90m (114in)**	Projectile weight: **14,250m (15,585 yards)**
Weight travelling: **6700kg (14,771lb)**	Armour: **n/a**
Weight in action: **5500kg (12,125lb)**	Engine: **n/a**
Elevation arc: **+5° to +60°**	Muzzle velocity: **600mps (1969fps)**
Traverse arc: **50°**	Speed: **n/a**

It was in the late 1920s that the Italian Army decided it needed a modern heavy howitzer. Although work on a new weapon began in 1930 with the Direzione Servizio Tecnici Armi e Munizioni supervising the efforts of the Ansaldo and OTO design teams, it was 1938 before the first 16 prototype and service trial examples of the Obice da 149/19 modello 37 (specification at left) appeared.

The Italian Army ordered 1392 production examples from Ansaldo and OTO, but only just under 150 weapons had been delivered by September 1943, the date Italy effectively quit the war on the Axis side, after which there was a modest increase in the production rate for the three variants of this howitzer, namely the modelli 37, 41 and 42 (greater elevation arc and range) that differed from each other only in minor details.

All three variants were of orthodox design and mounted on an unadventurous two-wheeled carriage of the split-trail type, and were thought by the Italians to be superior to equivalent Allied weapons. The production line was located in northern Italy, so after the partition of Italy following the armistice of September 1943, the Germans were able to keep the weapon in production for their own use with the revised designation 15cm schwere Feldhaubitze 404(i). This weapon was a reliable and robust heavy artillery piece.

GUN 210/22 MO 35

Created at the same time as the Cannone da 149/50 gun in the mid-1930s in an effort to provide the Italian Army's artillery arm with heavy equipment of modern capability, the Obice da 210/22 was designed by the army's own Servizio Tecnici Armi e Munizioni and manufactured by Ansaldo, although OTO was also involved at a later date. Orders for 346 such equipments had been placed by 1940, but by September 1942 only 20 were in operational service. The modello 35 was one of the finest items of Italian artillery as it offered an excellent combination of mobility, accuracy and weight of fire. The carriage was of the split-trail type and all four main wheels were lifted off the ground for firing, and once the trail spades had been lifted, the carriage and platform could be traversed through 360°. For movement the modello 35 was generally transported as two loads (barrel and carriage), but the equipment could be further broken down into four primary and one secondary loads, the latter for ancillary and assembly equipment. A number of these fine weapons were sold to Hungary for service with the local designation 21cm 39.M. An upgraded development made under licence were the 40.M and finally 40.aM standards, and after 1943 the Germans kept the 210/22 in Italian production as the 21cm Haubitze 520(i).

SPECIFICATIONS

GUN 210/22 MO 35

Type: **heavy towed howitzer**	Effective ceiling: **n/a**
Calibre: **210mm (8.269in)**	Road range: **n/a**
Vehicle length: **n/a**	Range: **15,400m (16,840 yards)**
Length of barrel: **5m (196.9in)**	Projectile weight: **133kg (293lb)**
Weight travelling: **unknown**	Armour: **n/a**
Weight in action: **15,885kg (35,020lb)**	Engine: **n/a**
Elevation arc: **0° to +70°**	Muzzle velocity: **560mps (1837fps)**
Traverse arc: **75–360°**	Speed: **n/a**

37MM GUN TYPE 94

SPECIFICATIONS

37MM GUN TYPE 94

Type:
light AT and support gun

Effective ceiling:
n/a

Calibre:
37mm (1.46in)

Road range:
n/a

Vehicle length:
n/a

Range:
4550m (4975 yards)

Length of barrel:
1.6865m (66.4in)

Projectile weight:
n/a

Weight travelling:
n/a

Armour:
n/a

Weight in action:
320kg (705.5lb)

Engine:
n/a

Elevation arc:
-10° to +27°

Muzzle velocity:
700mps (2297fps)

Traverse arc:
60°

Speed:
n/a

When it was introduced to service in 1934 (the Japanese year 2594, hence the designation), the 37mm Type 94 was meant to be an infantry weapon for use in the anti-tank and support roles. By 1941 the weapon's anti-tank capability was realized as wholly insufficient (it was capable of penetrating 24mm [.94in] of armour at a range of 900m [985 yards]), but the weapon was retained in service for lack of any replacement. The Japanese Army therefore used the weapon increasingly in the support role, though even then its performance was adequate at best.

In common with most other Japanese guns that entered service before World War II, the Type 94 was notably low in silhouette, light enough for easy manhandling on the battlefield (as can be seen above), although it was towed over longer distances by a vehicle or draught animals, and basically orthodox in its design. The large-diameter wheels were of the wooden-spoked or metal disc types, and the gun was anchored in firing position by spades hammered into the ground at the rear ends of the split trails. the split trails were anchored by spades which were driven down into the ground. The horizontally sliding breech block was of the semi-automatic type, and the gun was manually loaded. The above photograph shows a captured model in US use.

47MM ANTI-TANK GUN TYPE 1

The only anti-tank gun of wholly indigenous design to enter production for the Imperial Japanese Army, the 47mm Anti-tank Gun Type 1 was standardized for service during 1941 (hence the Type 1, or year 2601 designation). Designed by the army's own ordnance department and manufactured by its Osaka Arsenal, the Type 1 weapon had a fairly modern appearance but, by comparison with the anti-tank guns fielded by other world powers at this time, was somewhat lacking in overall performance as the Japanese themselves faced little armoured opposition in their war in China and felt that possible opponents of the future, most notably the Americans, British and Dutch, would operate only light tanks offering capabilities no better than the armoured vehicles of the Japanese Army. The Type 1 weapon had a semi-automatic breech block, which automatically opened and ejected the spent case after a round had been fired, and among its other features were a split-trail carriage with a shield and two wheels that were at first of the spoked wooden type with steel tyres but then of the steel type with pneumatic tyres. The Japanese used the Type 1 gun in most theatres, but most notably in Southeast Asia, and also developed the weapon as the Tank Gun Type 1 as the main armament of the Type 97 CHI-HA Medium Tank.

SPECIFICATIONS

47MM ANTI-TANK GUN

Type:
light towed AT gun

Calibre:
47mm (1.85in)

Vehicle length:
n/a

Length of barrel:
2.527m (99.5in)

Weight travelling:
n/a

Weight in action:
750kg (1653lb)

Elevation arc:
-11° to +19°

Traverse arc:
60°

Effective ceiling:
n/a

Road range:
n/a

Range:
460m (500 yards)

Projectile weight:
1.4kg (3.08lb)

Armour:
n/a

Engine:
n/a

Muzzle velocity:
825mps (2707fps)

Speed:
n/a

75MM PACK GUN TYPE 94

SPECIFICATIONS

75MM PACK GUN TYPE 94

Type: **light pack gun**	Effective ceiling: **n/a**
Calibre: **75mm (2.95in)**	Road range: **n/a**
Vehicle length: **n/a**	Range: **8175m (8940 yards)**
Length of barrel: **1.56m (61.5in)**	Projectile weight: **6.18kg (13.62lb)**
Weight travelling: **n/a**	Armour: **n/a**
Weight in action: **535kg (1179lb)**	Engine: **n/a**
Elevation arc: **-10° to +45°**	Muzzle velocity: **355mps (1165fps)**
Traverse arc: **40°**	Speed: **n/a**

The Japanese 75mm Mountain Gun Type 94, which was a pack weapon designed for easy breaking down into loads that could be carried by pack animals, was based on the Regimental Gun Type 41, another pack gun which the more modern weapon succeeded in service with the mountain artillery regiments of the Imperial Japanese Army from 1934.

By comparison with its predecessor, the Type 94 gun introduced a revised trail and a longer barrel characterized by a sliding breech block. The overall design was neatly conceived along modern lines, and the gun possessed considerable strength while it was also capable of being broken down, in a time of some 3 to 5 minutes, into 11 loads for carriage on 6 draught animals or by men: 18 men were adequate to move the loads over easy country, but more were necessary in difficult conditions. Once all 11 loads had arrived at the new firing position, the Type 94 gun could be put back together in some 10 minutes.

The Type 94 remained in service with the Imperial Japanese Army right to end of World War II in 1945. The weapon was also intended for use by the army's airborne arm, but appears not to have been employed in this task. The airborne arm was, in any case, deficient in troop- and equipment-carrying aircraft.

75MM AA GUN TYPE 88

Dating from 1928, the 75mm Mobile Field Anti-Aircraft Gun Type 88 was possibly produced in larger numbers than any other medium anti-aircraft gun for the Imperial Japanese Army. The weapon was allocated to virtually every anti-aircraft artillery field regiment to provide campaign forces with a high level of protection against medium-altitude air attack.

However, as World War II continued many of these equipments were withdrawn from field units and reallocated to regiments tasked with the defence of the Japanese home islands against air attack and, increasingly more probable from 1945 onwards, amphibious assault. Despite the importance of the weapon, the Type 88 gun was in fact produced only in modest numbers, for it was similar to other Japanese medium- and large-calibre weapons in being manufactured in a process requiring extensive machining. In overall capability the Type 88 gun was in no way exceptional, and for use was installed on a pedestal mounting stabilized on the ground by four outrigger legs. Had the weapons remained with ground forces they may have taken a large toll of American aircraft, but as it was they made little difference when it came to defending the home islands, which were being pounded by massive American air fleets.

SPECIFICATIONS

75MM AA GUN TYPE 88

Type:
medium towed AA gun

Calibre:
75mm (2.95in)

Vehicle length:
n/a

Length of barrel:
3.315m (130.5in)

Weight travelling:
2750kg (6063lb)

Weight in action:
2445kg (5390lb)

Elevation arc:
0° to +85°

Traverse arc:
360°

Effective ceiling:
7200m (23,620ft)

Road range:
n/a

Range:
n/a

Projectile weight:
6.58kg (14.5lb)

Armour:
n/a

Engine:
n/a

Muzzle velocity:
720mps (2362fps)

Speed:
n/a

75MM FIELD GUN TYPE 38

SPECIFICATIONS

75MM FIELD GUN TYPE 38

Type: **light towed gun**	Effective ceiling: **n/a**
Calibre: **75mm (2.95in)**	Road range: **n/a**
Vehicle length: **n/a**	Range: **11,975m (13,095 yards)**
Length of barrel: **2.285m (90in)**	Projectile weight: **6.025kg (13.27lb)**
Weight travelling: **1910kg (4211lb)**	Armour: **n/a**
Weight in action: **1135kg (2502lb)**	Engine: **n/a**
Elevation arc: **-8° to +43°**	Muzzle velocity: **605mps (1985fps)**
Traverse arc: **7°**	Speed: **n/a**

The origins of the 75mm Field Gun Type 38 (Improved) can be found in 1905, when the Imperial Japanese Army selected a light field gun of Krupp design as the basis of its Field Gun Type 38 that was manufactured at the army's own Osaka Arsenal for service from 1906.

During World War I, in which the only extensive use of Japanese artillery took place in the siege and capture of the German treaty port of Tsingtao in China, most of the equipments were cycled through a modernization programme at the Osaka Arsenal to re-emerge as much modernized Type 38 (Improved) guns in which the original type of box trail gave way to an open box trail giving a greater maximum elevation angle, and the gun's mounting on its carriage was much improved. The Type 38 (Improved) gun was still in large-scale army service as Japan entered World War II in December 1941, having apparently proved its continued viability during the ongoing campaign in China. Experience soon revealed that the Type 38 (Improved) gun was decidedly inferior to American and British field artillery, however, but for lack of adequate numbers of more modern weapons, it continued in service as the standard gun of divisional artillery regiments right through to the end of World War II in 1945.

75MM FIELD GUN TYPE 90

The most advanced item of light field artillery equipment available to the Japanese Army in World War II was the 75mm Field Gun Type 90. This entered service in 1930 under conditions of great secrecy as the Japanese thought that the weapon would confer significant tactical advantages against enemies who knew nothing of the type.

In design the Type 90 was akin to the Canon de 85 modèle 1927 supplied to Greece by the French armaments manufacturer Schneider, and it is probable that the basic concept of the gun was copied by the Japanese rather than produced under licence. Manufacture was the responsibility of the Japanese Army's own Osaka Arsenal, and while the first examples used the Schneider type of breech, the later weapons were revised with a breech of the sliding wedge type. The equipment was also produced with large-diameter wooden spoked wheels that were later succeeded by smaller wheels with pneumatic rubber tyres to suit the Type 90 to motor towing. The first knowledge of the Type 90 outside Japan came to light during 1940, when the weapon was first used in China. Although China and Manchuria were the theatres that absorbed most of Type 92 production, the weapon was also used in Malaya during 1942.

SPECIFICATIONS

75MM FIELD GUN TYPE 90

Type:
light towed field gun

Effective ceiling:
n/a

Calibre:
75mm (2.95in)

Road range:
n/a

Vehicle length:
n/a

Range:
15,000m (16,405 yards)

Length of barrel:
2.855m (112.4in)

Projectile weight:
6.025kg (13.27lb)

Weight travelling:
2000kg (4405lb)

Armour:
n/a

Weight in action:
1400kg (3086lb)

Engine:
n/a

Elevation arc:
-8° to +43°

Muzzle velocity:
700mps (2297fps)

Traverse arc:
50°

Speed:
n/a

105MM HOWITZER TYPE 91

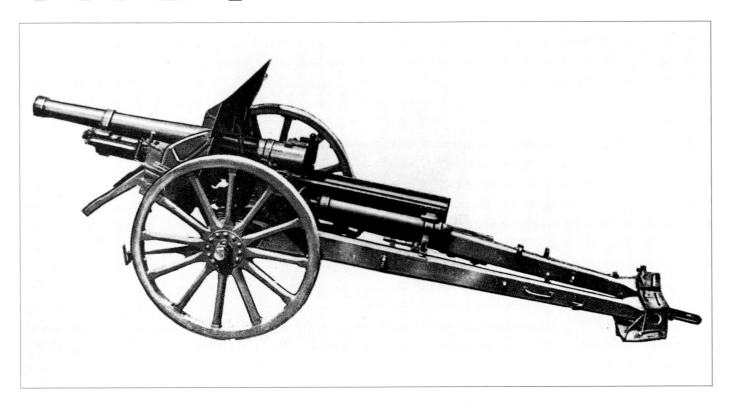

SPECIFICATIONS

105MM HOWITZER TYPE 91

Type:
  medium towed howitzer

Calibre:
  105mm (4.13in)

Vehicle length:
  n/a

Length of barrel:
  2.54m (100in)

Weight travelling:
  1980kg (4365lb)

Weight in action:
  150kg (3307lb)

Elevation arc:
  -5° to +45°

Traverse arc:
  45°

Effective ceiling:
  n/a

Road range:
  n/a

Range:
  10,775m (11,785 yards)

Projectile weight:
  15.77kg (34.7lb)

Armour:
  n/a

Engine:
  n/a

Muzzle velocity:
  545mps (1788fps)

Speed:
  n/a

As part of Japan's policy of assessing the best of foreign weapons to ensure that it kept abreast of the latest technical developments in the world's most advanced industrial nations, a Japanese mission in France during the later part of the 1920s ordered for evaluation a limited batch of Schneider 105mm field gun/howitzers. When delivered to Japan, these gun/howitzers were thoroughly evaluated in their tactical and technical aspects, and the Japanese then embarked on the design of a gun that embodied all the best features found in the French weapon. The result was the 105mm Howitzer Type 91, which was manufactured at the army's own Osaka Arsenal to enter prototype trials in 1929 and full service from 1931.

Despite the fact that the weapon was notably unsophisticated in its finish (a feature of all Osaka-produced weapons), it was structurally light without sacrificing sturdiness and reliability, qualities that would stand it in good stead during the army's campaigns in the jungles of Southeast Asia. As a result of its durable qualities, the weapon proved popular with the men of the Japanese Army's artillery regiments, and served as a standard piece of divisional artillery equipment right through World War II, also proving a sound weapon on the battlefield.

40MM BOFORS GUN

Without doubt the 40mm Bofors gun, designed in a country that remained neutral, was the most widely employed anti-aircraft gun of World War II. The first weapon appeared in 1930 after the Bofors company had received financial backing from the Swedish government for a design of 1928, and the first weapons were produced as single mountings on wheeled carriages for land service, and twin mountings on fixed mountings for naval service. Fed from an overhead hopper loaded by means of four-round clips, the weapon was exported and built under licence from 1932, and by 1939 the Bofors gun was in service with some 18 countries, some of which introduced significant changes and also exported the revised weapon.

The British produced three marks of the gun for use on six mountings and five firing platforms, and there were also one-, two- and four-barrel naval mountings. The USA adopted the weapon in 1941 as the 40mm Anti-aircraft Gun M1 that was installed on a number of mountings, and also developed manually operated single mountings as well as power-operated mountings with two and four barrels (sometimes with radar control) for naval use. The specification applies to the British Gun Mk 1 on Mk 3 Mounting and Mk 2 Platform. The British version is shown above.

SPECIFICATIONS

40MM BOFORS GUN

Type: **medium towed AA gun**	Effective ceiling: **7200m (23,600ft)**
Calibre: **40mm (1.575in)**	Road range: **n/a**
Vehicle length: **n/a**	Range: **n/a**
Length of barrel: **2.249mm (88.58in)**	Projectile weight: **0.89kg (1.96lb)**
Weight travelling: **2460kg (5423lb)**	Armour: **n/a**
Weight in action: **unknown**	Engine: **n/a**
Elevation arc: **-5° to +90°**	Muzzle velocity: **854mps (2800fps)**
Traverse arc: **360°**	Speed: **n/a**

37/MM AA GUN M1

SPECIFICATIONS

37MM AA GUN M1

Type: **light towed AA gun**	Effective ceiling: **5670m (18,600ft)**
Calibre: **37mm (1.457 in)**	Road range: **n/a**
Vehicle length: **n/a**	Range: **n/a**
Length of barrel: **1.9m (78in)**	Projectile weight: **0.61kg (1lb 5.5oz)**
Weight travelling: **2778kg (6125lb)**	Armour: **n/a**
Weight in action: **unknown**	Engine: **n/a**
Elevation arc: **-5° to +90°**	Muzzle velocity: **853mps (2800fps)**
Traverse arc: **360°**	Speed: **n/a**

It was in 1921 that the celebrated designer John Browning began work on the development of a 37mm anti-aircraft gun, but this effort came to a halt with the designer's death in 1926. It was only in 1935 that work was re-started to finalize the weapon that served with the US Army Air Forces as the 37mm Aircraft Automatic Gun M4 and M10, the US Navy as the 37mm M4, and the US Army as the Anti-aircraft Gun M1 that was later developed into the M1A2.

These guns differed from each other only in minor details. The M1 entered service in 1940 and though, soon after this, the Americans decided to standardize the Bofors as the 40mm Gun M1, production of this superior weapon could not meet demand. As a result Colt continued production of the 37mm M1, of which 7278 were completed. This Browning gun thus served right through the USA's involvement in World War II, and saw action on every American front.

The weapon was supplied with ammunition from the left in the form of single rounds or 10-round clips, and could fire either single rounds or in automatic mode. The carriage was a straightforward platform which could be lowered from its four wheels and stabilized by two folding. It had a rate of fire of 120 rounds per minute and fired high explosive ammunition.

37MM AT GUN M3

The USA's 37mm Anti-tank Gun M3 was derived from the 3.7cm PaK 36/36 produced in Germany by Rheinmetall-Borsig, but introduced a number of changes thought desirable by the US Army. Considering that the German weapon became obsolete quite quickly following the outbreak of World War II this was very prudent.

The M3 was lighter than the PaK 35/36 as a result of its Carriage M4 (later M4A1), and to help control the recoil forces a five-baffle muzzle brake was added. Although it was soon learned that the muzzle brake was not needed, all but the first few guns were fitted for – if not with – such a brake to create the M3A1 standard. After 1941 the 37mm calibre was next to useless in European combat, so most of the 18,702 such weapons were used in the Pacific theatre, where they were used for infantry support firing HE and canister rounds.

The M3A1 served with the US forces right through World War II, and was widely allocated to Allied nations during and after the war. The gun was widely used as the primary armament of light tanks and armoured cars, and was also tested in a number of self-propelled mountings none of which was standardized for full service. That it was still in service at the end of the war indicates that the changes made at the beginning of its life paid dividends in later years.

SPECIFICATIONS

37MM AT GUN M3

Type: **light towed AT gun**	Effective ceiling: **n/a**
Calibre: **37mm (1.46in)**	Road range: **n/a**
Vehicle length: **n/a**	Range: **915m (1000 yards)**
Length of barrel: **1.9m (78in)**	Projectile weight: **0.87kg (1lb 14.75oz)**
Weight travelling: **414kg (912lb)**	Armour: **n/a**
Weight in action: **unknown**	Engine: **n/a**
Elevation arc: **-10° to +15°**	Muzzle velocity: **884mps (2900fps)**
Traverse arc: **60°**	Speed: **n/a**

57MM ANTI-TANK GUN M1

SPECIFICATIONS

57MM ANTI-TANK GUN M1

Type: **medium towed AT gun**	Effective ceiling: **n/a**
Calibre: **57mm (2.244in)**	Road range: **n/a**
Vehicle length: **n/a**	Range: **915m (1000 yards)**
Length of barrel: **2.97m (117in)**	Projectile weight: **2.8kg (6.28lb)**
Weight travelling: **1225kg (2700lb)**	Armour: **n/a**
Weight in action: **unknown**	Engine: **n/a**
Elevation arc: **-5° to +15°**	Muzzle velocity: **823mps (2700fps)**
Traverse arc: **90°**	Speed: **n/a**

As its experts watched the progress of operations in Europe and North Africa in 1941, when the USA was still neutral, the USA decided that its 37mm anti-tank gun was obsolete (as the Germans discovered with their own weapon of the same calibre when the rounds bounced off the hulls of enemy tanks) and that the surest way to get an effective weapon into service was the licensed production of the British 6-pdr weapon.

From February 1941 the American revised the British plans to suit US production practices, and the result was the 57mm Anti tank Gun M1 - Carriage M1. The carriage differed from the British original principally in using a wheel-operated traverse system, but was then modified, firstly by fitting combat tyres to produce the M1A1, secondly by reverting to the British shoulder-operated free traverse to produce the M1A2, and thirdly by making changes to the towing eye to create the M1A3.

The 57mm gun was used on a large scale throughout World War II, but its most important application was as a self-propelled gun supplied under the terms of the Lease-Lend Act to the British and the Soviets on the Eastern Front, where it filled a large gap created by the loss of thousands of guns captured by the Germans. This was the Gun Motor Carriage T48 on the M3 halftrack vehicle, and 962 guns were produced for this task.

75MM PACK HOWITZER M1

Work on the item that matured as the 75mm Pack Howitzer M1A1 started during 1920, and the weapon was standardized as the M1 in 1927. Slight changes to the breech ring and block were then effected to create the M1A1. The barrel was installed on the Carriage M1 with tyreless spoked wheels and designed for mountain warfare, and the equipment could be broken down into six loads.

In overall terms the equipment was modern in design and strong in construction, and an unusual aspect was provided by the fact that the traverse handwheel worked directly on the axle, allowing the cradle to carry only the elevation gear. A slow initial production rate meant that just under 100 such equipments were in service by the middle of 1940, but by the time of the USA's entry into World War II in December 1941 there were slightly more than 450 in service and total production was 4939 by the end of the war. Modernization of the carriage with pneumatically tyred wheels and provision for paradropping (nine loads) created the Carriage M8, whose overall weight was 608kg (1340lb). The M8 gradually replaced the M1 carriage, and the type was issued to many Allied forces including the British, who operated a version for amphibious forces as the 75mm Pack Howitzer Mk I.

SPECIFICATIONS

75MM PACK HOWITZER M1

Type: **light towed howitzer**	Effective ceiling: **n/a**
Calibre: **75mm (2.95 in)**	Road range: **n/a**
Vehicle length: **n/a**	Range: **8915m (9750 yards)**
Length of barrel: **1.19m (47in)**	Projectile weight: **6.242kg (13.76lb)**
Weight travelling: **588kg (1296lb)**	Armour: **n/a**
Weight in action: **unknown**	Engine: **n/a**
Elevation arc: **-5° to +45°**	Muzzle velocity: **381mps (1250fps)**
Traverse arc: **6°**	Speed: **n/a**

HELLCAT

SPECIFICATIONS

HELLCAT

Type:
76mm SP AT gun

Effective ceiling:
n/a

Calibre:
n/a

Road range:
241km (150 miles)

Vehicle length:
5.38m (17ft 4in)

Range:
n/a

Length of barrel:
n/a

Projectile weight:
n/a

Weight travelling:
n/a

Armour:
7–12mm (.28–.47in)

Weight in action:
17,999kg (39,680lb)

Engine:
Continental R-975-C4

Elevation arc:
n/a

Muzzle velocity:
n/a

Traverse arc:
n/a

Speed:
80km/h (50mph)

Standardized in February 1944, the five-man 76mm Gun Motor Carriage M18, which gained the nickname Hellcat in service, was one of the most successful tank destroyers to see operational service in World War II. Although it was only lightly protected by armour, the M18 was fast and mobile, and was greatly aided by its low silhouette. The primary armament, complemented by a single 0.5in Browning M2HB machine gun for local defence, was the 76mm M1A1 or M1A2 high-velocity gun. This was installed in an open-topped turret providing 360° traverse, and the mounting allowed an elevation arc between -10° to +19°.

Ammunition capacity was 45 rounds for the main gun and 1000 rounds for the machine gun. The M62 armour-piercing projectile fired by the main gun left the barrel at 792m (2600ft) per second and could puncture 102mm (4in) of armour at 90m (100 yards). The chassis of the Gun Motor Carriage M18 was based on what was basically a new type of light tank chassis with torsion-bar suspension that was considerably superior in many respects to the vertical volute suspension typical of American medium tanks of the period and used in the Gun Motor Carriages M10 and M36 using the chassis of the M4 Sherman tank.

3IN ANTI-TANK GUN M5

Late in 1942 the US Army sought to create an indigenous weapon to replace the obsolescent 57mm M1 gun that was a licence-built version of the British 6-pdr anti-tank gun. Rather than attempt the lengthy process of creating an entirely new weapon, the Americans opted for the expedient of combining elements of the hardware embodied in other guns. Thus the barrel was that of the 76.2mm M3 anti-aircraft gun, while the breech, recoil system and carriage were those of the 105mm M2A1 howitzer. In its new guise the carriage became the 3in Gun Carriage M1, which was later developed into the 3in Gun Carriage M6. The Anti-tank Gun M5 – Carriage M1 that resulted from this process was large and somewhat unwieldy weapon that, in common with a number of other improvised weapons that appeared in World War II, could be developed and produced without delay and had the major attribute of working well. The M5 anti-tank gun was employed in every theatre in which American troops fought, and for its reliability and good punch became a well-liked weapon. The same basic gun was adapted as the M7 for use in the Gun Motor Carriage M10, which was a very successful tank destroyer. Overall production amounted to some 2500 examples of the M5 and another 6824 examples of the M10.

SPECIFICATIONS

3IN ANTI-TANK GUN M5

Type: **medium towed AT gun**	*Effective ceiling:* **n/a**
Calibre: **76.2mm (3in)**	*Road range:* **n/a**
Vehicle length: **n/a**	*Range:* **915m (1000 yards)**
Length of barrel: **4.023m (158.4in)**	*Projectile weight:* **6.94kg (15.43lb)**
Weight travelling: **2654kg (5850lb)**	*Armour:* **n/a**
Weight in action: **n/a**	*Engine:* **n/a**
Elevation arc: **-5° to +30°**	*Muzzle velocity:* **792mps (2600fps)**
Traverse arc: **46°**	*Speed:* **n/a**

M10 TANK DESTROYER

SPECIFICATIONS

M10 TANK DESTROYER

Type: **medium tank destroyer**	Effective ceiling: **n/a**
Calibre: **n/a**	Road range: **322km (200 miles)**
Vehicle length: **5.97m (19ft 7in)**	Range: **n/a**
Length of barrel: **n/a**	Projectile weight: **n/a**
Weight travelling: **29,699kg (65,475lb)**	Armour: **12–37mm (.47–1.96in)**
Weight in action: **n/a**	Engine: **GM 6-71-6046 x 2**
Elevation arc: **n/a**	Muzzle velocity: **n/a**
Traverse arc: **n/a**	Speed: **48km/h (30mph)**

The five-man 3in Gun Motor Carriage M10 was the first tank destroyer developed for the US Army on the basis of a fully tracked rather than halftracked chassis. Work on the creation of this important weapon began in April 1942, and progressed so well that the resulting M10 was standardized in June of the same year. The Gun Motor Carriage M10 comprised the 3in Anti-tank Gun M7 mounted in a 360° traverse turret with an only partially covered top on the chassis of the Medium Tank M4A2 Sherman.

The anti-tank gun could be elevated in an arc between -10° and +19°, and was provided with 54 rounds of APC and HE ammunition, the former firing its projectile with a muzzle velocity of 792m (2600ft) per second to penetrate 102mm (4in) of face-hardened armour at 915m (1000 yards). The turret also carried one 12.7mm (0.5in) Browning M2HB machine gun (300 rounds) for local defence and protection against attacks by low-flying warplanes. The M10's armour protection could be increased by attaching auxiliary armour of differing thickness to the basic armour.

The M10A1 variant was a training vehicle used only in the USA and differed from the M10 in being based on the chassis of the M4A3 Sherman tank with a single Ford GAA engine.

90MM AA GUN M1

Schemed as the modern replacement for the obsolescent 3in Anti-aircraft Gun M3, the 90mm Anti-aircraft Gun M1 was placed in development during June 1938 as the 90mm Anti-aircraft Gun T2, work on the complementary Mount T1 starting only a short time later. Both the gun and the mount were standardized for US Army service in the course of March 1940.

The 90mm Anti-aircraft Gun M1 was planned as a dedicated air defence weapon with no dual-role capability to allow use in the anti-tank role as was possible with weapons such as the Germans' 8.8cm FlaK weapons. The gun was therefore installed on a platform mount with a cruciform arrangement of stabilizing outrigger legs which could be folded for transport on only two road wheels. The M1A1 was identical to the M1 apart from its provision for installation of the Spring Rammer M8 to facilitate loading.

Drawing up plans for this weapon was easier than the actual manufacture, and production of the M1 and M1A1 was initially slow, largely as a result of the gun's complexity and the fine tolerances needed in the creation of the all-important fire-control system. Despite the weapon's creation for single-role service, some M1 guns were installed on M3 mounts and used as coast defence weapons.

SPECIFICATIONS

90MM AA GUN M1

Type: **heavy towed AA gun**	Effective ceiling: **12,040m (39,50 ft)**
Calibre: **90mm (3.54in)**	Road range: **n/a**
Vehicle length: **n/a**	Range: **n/a**
Length of barrel: **4.737m (186.5in)**	Projectile weight: **10.62kg (23.415lb)**
Weight travelling: **8618kg (19,000lb)**	Armour: **n/a**
Weight in action: **unknown**	Engine: **n/a**
Elevation arc: **0° to +80°**	Muzzle velocity: **823mps (2700fps)**
Traverse arc: **360°**	Speed: **n/a**

105MM FIELD HOWITZER M2

SPECIFICATIONS

105MM FIELD HOWITZER M2

Type:
medium towed howitzer

Effective ceiling:
n/a

Calibre:
105mm (4.13in)

Road range:
n/a

Vehicle length:
n/a

Range:
11,430m (12,500 yards)

Length of barrel:
2.574m (101.35in)

Projectile weight:
14.97kg (33lb)

Weight travelling:
1932kg (4260lb)

Armour:
n/a

Weight in action:
n/a

Engine:
n/a

Elevation arc:
-5° to +65°

Muzzle velocity:
472mps (1550fps)

Traverse arc:
46°

Speed:
n/a

The core of the US Army's field artillery capability in World War II was the 105mm Howitzer M2. This was one of the weapons recommended by the board that was established in 1919 to assess artillery performance in World War I and make recommendations for across-the-board improvements, but progress toward the creation of new weapons was slowed by the financial retrenchment that followed World War I, the world financial crisis of the late 1920s and early 1930s, and the USA's increasing isolationism. Thus it was only in 1939 that the design of the new howitzer was completed by the Bureau of Ordnance, and production of the weapon began in 1940 at the start of a programme that saw the delivery of 8536 such 105mm Howitzer M2A1 equipments in the course of World War II. The Carriage M2A2 was of the split-trail type with two pneumatically tyred wheels, and was of notably reliable design and sturdy manufacture. The barrel of this successful and popular weapon, which was used in all American theatres, could be used to fire 13 types of ammunition, a fact that greatly enhanced its tactical flexibility. The howitzer was also installed on a number of mobile mounts, the most notable combination being the 105mm Howitzer Motor Carriage M7, known to the British as the Priest, on the chassis of the M3 and M4 medium tanks.

105MM HOWITZER M7

One of the most important developments in artillery during World War II was the fielding of self-propelled guns and howitzers to support armoured and motorized formations. Such equipments were based on chassis types capable of providing the same cross country performance and the forces they were designed to aid, and the 105mm Howitzer M2A1 (known to the British as the Priest) remains a classic example. The seven-man 105mm Howitzer Motor Carriage M7 was based on the chassis of the M3 medium tank. This was standardized in April 1942 and, after the M3 tank had been phased out of production, further development was centred on the M7B series using the chassis of the closely related M4 medium tank. The two models were the M7B1 based on the M4A3 with the Ford GAA engine and the M7B2 based on the M4A4 with the Chrysler 5-521 multi-bank engine. The tank turret was omitted and the superstructure was raised to create an open-topped fighting compartment, with a "pulpit" mounting on its right-hand forward corner for a 0.5in Browning M2HB local defence machine gun with 300 rounds. Supplied with 69 rounds, the howitzer was in the front of the fighting compartment on a mounting that allowed elevation through an arc between -5° and +33° as well as traverse 12° left and 25° right of the centreline.

SPECIFICATIONS

105MM HOWITZER M7

Type: **medium SP howitzer**	Effective ceiling: **n/a**
Calibre: **n/a**	Road range: **200km (125 miles)**
Vehicle length: **6.02m (19ft 9in)**	Range: **n/a**
Length of barrel: **n/a**	Projectile weight: **n/a**
Weight travelling: **n/a**	Armour: **12.7–114mm (.5–4.5in)**
Weight in action: **22,967kg (50,634lb)**	Engine: **Continental R-975**
Elevation arc: **n/a**	Muzzle velocity: **n/a**
Traverse arc: **n/a**	Speed: **42km/h (26mph)**

155MM HOWITZER M1

SPECIFICATIONS

155MM HOWITZER M1

Type:
heavy towed howitzer

Effective ceiling:
n/a

Calibre:
155mm (6.1in)

Road range:
n/a

Vehicle length:
n/a

Range:
14,630m (16,000 yards)

Length of barrel:
3.81m (150in)

Projectile weight:
43.14kg (95lb)

Weight travelling:
5428kg (11,966lb)

Armour:
n/a

Weight in action:
unknown

Engine:
n/a

Elevation arc:
-2° to +65°

Muzzle velocity:
564mps (1850fps)

Traverse arc:
53°

Speed:
n/a

It was in 1939 that work began on the design and development of a new heavy howitzer for the US Army, this 155mm Howitzer M1 being created at the Rock Island Arsenal. For obvious reasons of standardization and reduced spares holdings, it was planned that the new equipment should use the carriage as that for the 4.5in Gun M1, and as events turned out the howitzer was manufactured in considerably greater numbers than the tactically less useful gun.

The M1 howitzer entered service in 1942, and by the end of World War II in 1945 some 4035 such equipments had been built. The M1 howitzer was a highly successful and very popular weapon that possessed an enviable reputation for accuracy. In basic design the howitzer was conventional, and for firing the Carriage M1 (of the split-trail type) was stabilized by a jack under the axle. Improved versions of the equipment were the Carriages M1A1 and M1A2 with different firing jacks, while a later version of the howitzer was the 155mm Howitzer M1A1 made of a stronger steel. The sole self-propelled mounting was the 155mm Howitzer Motor Carriage M41 "Gorilla". Like most American heavy artillery pieces, the M1 howitzer was robust and reliable, and packed a powerful punch. Such weapons aided the victories over both Germany and Japan.

8IN HOWITZER M1

Like the 155mm Gun M1, the 8in Howitzer M1 was a development of an existing weapon, specifically the 8in Howitzer Mks VI to VIII, which were British equipments initially provided to the US Army by the British in 1917 and 1918 during World War I, and then manufactured under licence in the USA.

By 1940 the original-pattern weapons were decidedly long in the tooth and being phased out of service with the US Army that was in the process of preparing for service a new 203mm (8in) howitzer under development from the original weapon by the Hughes Tool Company. The new 8in Howitzer M1 in fact entered service during in 1942, and the equipment used the same breech mechanism and carriage as the 155mm Gun M1. Manufacture of 1006 such equipments had been completed before the end of World War II in 1945. In service the 8in Howitzer M1 was a popular weapon that was especially notable for its accuracy and capability in tasks such as the reduction of fortifications, qualities that were especially needed in northwest Europe against the Siegfried Line and in Italy, where the Germans built a number of strong defence lines among the many hills and in the mountainous terrain. The only self-propelled version of this impressive weapon was the 8in Howitzer Motor Carriage M43.

SPECIFICATIONS

8IN HOWITZER M1

Type:
heavy towed howitzer

Calibre:
203.2mm (8in)

Vehicle length:
n/a

Length of barrel:
n/a

Weight travelling:
14,515kg (32,000lb)

Weight in action:
13,4672kg (29,700lb)

Elevation arc:
-2° to +64°

Traverse arc:
60°

Effective ceiling:
n/a

Road range:
n/a

Range:
16,915m (18,500 yards)

Projectile weight:
90.8kg (200lb)

Armour:
n/a

Engine:
n/a

Muzzle velocity:
594mps (1950fps)

Speed:
n/a

8IN GUN M1

SPECIFICATIONS

8IN GUN M1

Type: **heavy mobile gun**	Effective ceiling: **n/a**
Calibre: **203.2mm (8in)**	Road range: **n/a**
Vehicle length: **n/a**	Range: **32,005m (35,000 yards)**
Length of barrel: **10.401m (409.5in)**	Projectile weight: **109.13kg (240.37lb)**
Weight travelling: **31,434kg (69,300lb)**	Armour: **n/a**
Weight in action: **unknown**	Engine: **n/a**
Elevation arc: **-10° to +50°**	Muzzle velocity: **899mps (2950fps)**
Traverse arc: **40°**	Speed: **n/a**

The lessons of World War I on the Western Front, as they pertained to long-range artillery work, were reflected in the USA by the recommendations of the Calibre Board established in 1919 to consider the US Army's artillery needs. The board considered that a thoroughly modern long-range gun of 203mm (8in) calibre was needed, but the USA's worsening economic situation meant that work on the new weapon was suspended in 1924 and resumed only in 1939 for the first firing of the T2 prototype weapon in 1941, the year in which the new weapon was standardized for service as the 8in Gun M1. This was planned for use of the same Carriage M1 as the 240mm Howitzer M1, but the need for limited modifications meant that the carriage for the gun became the Carriage M2. The 8in Gun M1 entered service during 1942, and only 139 such equipments had been completed before the end of World War II in 1945 as the weapon was very large, heavy and costly. Movement was possible only on special wagons (one for the gun and its mounting, and another for the split trail required to handle the recoil forces) generally towed by converted M3 tanks, and the equipment had to be assembled in firing position with the aid of a truck-mounted crane. The M1 had an initial rate of fire of one round per minute, declining to one round per two minutes after 10 minutes.

45MM ANTI-TANK GUN 1942

The 45mm Anti-Tank Gun Model 1932 was in essence a scaled-up version of the 3.7cm PaK 35/36. The L/46 gun was installed on either of two carriages (for horse and motor traction) with two wire-spoked wheels. Despite its lightness, the Model 1932 was a capable weapon, and the Germans used captured examples with the designation 4.5cm PaK 184(r). The improved Model 1937 was almost identical and in German use became the 4.5cm PaK 184/1(r). A development of the Model 1937 was the Model 1938 tank gun which, in an effort to create more anti-tank guns in the disastrous days of 1941–43 on the Eastern Front, was installed on an interim carriage to create a weapon known to the German Army as the 4.5cm PaK 184/6(r).

To meet the problem of defeating the increasing thickness of tank armour in the early 1940s, the Soviets opted in the shorter term not to adopt a larger calibre but to increase the length of the 45mm barrel as a means of boosting muzzle velocity and this armour penetration from the Model 32 family's figure of 38mm (1.5in) at 915m (1000 yards) at 30°. The breech block was also strengthened and disc wheels were introduced in the 45mm Anti-Tank Gun Model 42 (specifications at right), which remained in Soviet service until well after World War II.

SPECIFICATIONS

45MM ANTI-TANK GUN 1942

Type: **light towed AT gun**	Effective ceiling: **n/a**
Calibre: **45mm (1.77in)**	Road range: **n/a**
Vehicle length: **n/a**	Range: **unknown**
Length of barrel: **2.967m (116.8in)**	Projectile weight: **1.43kg (3.15lb)**
Weight travelling: **unknown**	Armour: **n/a**
Weight in action: **570kg (1257lb)**	Engine: **n/a**
Elevation arc: **-8° to +25°**	Muzzle velocity: **820mps (2690fps)**
Traverse arc: **60°**	Speed: **n/a**

76.2MM AA GUN 1931 AND 1938

SPECIFICATIONS

76.2MM AA GUN 1931

Type:
medium towed AA gun

Effective ceiling:
9300m (30,510ft)

Calibre:
76.2mm (3in)

Road range:
n/a

Vehicle length:
n/a

Range:
n/a

Length of barrel:
4.19m (165in)

Projectile weight:
6.61kg (14.575lb)

Weight travelling:
4210kg (9281lb)

Armour:
n/a

Weight in action:
3050kg (6724lb)

Engine:
n/a

Elevation arc:
-3° to +82°

Muzzle velocity:
815 mps (2674fps)

Traverse arc:
360°

Speed:
n/a

The 76.2mm Anti-Aircraft Gun Model 1931 was one of the oldest anti-aircraft guns still in service with the Soviet forces at the time of the German invasion in June 1941 and, in common with many other such guns of the period, incorporated a number of design features related to Vickers' design thinking from the late 1920s. The gun was installed on a two-wheeled carriage for relatively good mobility, and was essentially straightforward in its handling and firing requirements.

The Germans captured large numbers in 1941 and 1942, and these entered German home defence service with the revised designation 7.62cm FlaK M31(r): when stocks of Soviet ammunition were exhausted, a few of the guns were rebored for German 88mm ammunition as 7.62/8.8cm FlaK M31(r) weapons, the last being scrapped in 1944. During 1938 the Soviets introduced a revised and updated version as the Anti-Aircraft Gun Model 1938 (specification at left) with a detachment of 11 (commander and 10 men), a two-axle carriage, and detail improvements to the gun and its controls. Captured examples of the Model 38 entered service as 7.62cm FlaK M38(r) or, after being rebored, 7.62/8.8cm FlaK M38(r) weapons. Both the Soviet and German weapons remained in service to the end of World War II.

76.2MM INFANTRY GUN 1943

The 76.2mm Infantry Gun Model 1927 (76–27) was a notably capable Soviet equipment that was produced in large numbers. The design was simple but efficient, like much Red Army hardware that saw service in World War II, and the large-diameter wheels provided a measure of lateral protection for the gun's detachment.

Between 1941 and 1942 large numbers of these weapons were captured by the Germans and placed in service with the designation 7.62cm Infantriekanonehaubitze 290(r). The Red Army lost literally thousands of artillery pieces, many of which were turned against their former masters. Vast amounts of ammunition for the guns also fell into the hands of the Germans during the early phase of Operation Barbarossa, the German invasion of the Soviet Union in June 1941.

In 1943 the Soviets introduced an updated gun as the 76.2mm Infantry Gun Model 1943 (76–43) that was in essence a modified 76–27 gun on the carriage of the 45mm anti-tank gun. The revised carriage resulted in a considerable lowering of weight from the 76–27's figure of 780kg (1720lb), with consequent advantages in general mobility and speed into and out of action, and also increased the traverse arc from the 76–27's figure of 6°. This improved the 76–43's capability in the anti-tank role, for which a hollow-charge projectile was provided.

SPECIFICATIONS

76.2MM INFANTRY GUN 1943

Type: **medium support gun**	Effective ceiling: **n/a**
Calibre: **76.2mm (3in)**	Road range: **n/a**
Vehicle length: **n/a**	Range: **8550m (9350 yards)**
Length of barrel: **1.257m (49.5in)**	Projectile weight: **6.21kg (13.69lb)**
Weight travelling: **n/a**	Armour: **n/a**
Weight in action: **600kg (1323lb)**	Engine: **n/a**
Elevation arc: **-8° to +25°**	Muzzle velocity: **387mps (1270fps)**
Traverse arc: **60°**	Speed: **n/a**

76.2MM FIELD GUN 1941

SPECIFICATIONS

76.2MM FIELD GUN 1941

Type: **light towed gun**	Effective ceiling: **n/a**
Calibre: **76.2mm (3in)**	Road range: **n/a**
Vehicle length: **n/a**	Range: **13,000m (14,215 yards)**
Length of barrel: **3.194mm (125.76in)**	Projectile weight: **6.21kg (13.69lb)**
Weight travelling: **1110kg (2447lb)**	Armour: **n/a**
Weight in action: **unknown**	Engine: **n/a**
Elevation arc: **-10° to +18°**	Muzzle velocity: **680mps (2231fps)**
Traverse arc: **56°**	Speed: **n/a**

The 76.2mm calibre had been standard for Russian and, from 1917, Soviet medium field artillery since the end of the eighteenth century. When the German invasion of 22 June 1941 drew the Soviet Union into World War II, the Soviet Red Army still numbered in its inventory a number of older weapons in this calibre, including the obsolescent Field Gun Models 00/02P, 02/26 and 02/30 together with the interim Model 1933 and the more modern Models 1936 (76–36) and 1939 (76–39).

By the end of 1941 the Soviets had suffered huge losses to the Germans, these losses including a high proportion of their field artillery. Urgent replenishment was the order of the day, and the first result was the 76.2mm Field Gun Model 1941/SiS 3 (76–41). This was the ordnance of the Model 1939 mounted on the 57mm Anti-tank Gun Model 1941/SiS 3's carriage as this was strong enough to handle the recoil of the larger-calibre but lower-velocity field gun, especially after the field gun had been fitted with a double-baffle muzzle brake and had its recoil system adapted.

The weapon was essentially an interim type, and only a comparatively small number were completed. The Germans used captured examples with the designation 7.62cm Feldkanone 288/1(r).

76.2MM FIELD GUN 1942

By 1942 the threat of imminent defeat had been lifted from the USSR following the defeat of the German Army before the gates of Moscow in December 1941 and the general Soviet offensive along the whole of the Eastern Front that followed. The Soviet authorities were now free to plan the creation and manufacture of the definitive weapons with which to encompass the total defeat of Germany.

By this time the Soviet Army had considerable experience in the use of 76.2mm field artillery, including older weapons as well as the extemporized Model 1941/SiS 3 (76–41) and less capable Model 1939/42 (76–39/42) on a new but lighter carriage, and this experience was combined into the 76.2mm Field Gun Model 1942/SiS 3 (76–42). This was basically the Model 1939 gun modified with a double-baffle muzzle brake and installed on a new carriage with a shield and split pole trails.

The 76–42 entered service late in 1942 and soon proved itself a reliable and capable light field gun that gained quick popularity with its users. Large-scale production was undertaken, and the Germans were only too happy to take captured examples of the equipment into their own service with the designation 7.62cm Feldkanone 288(r).

SPECIFICATIONS

76.2MM FIELD GUN 1942

Type: **light towed gun**	Effective ceiling: **n/a**
Calibre: **76.2mm (3in)**	Road range: **n/a**
Vehicle length: **n/a**	Range: **13,300m (14,545 yards)**
Length of barrel: **2.994m (117.87in)**	Projectile weight: **6.21kg (13.69lb)**
Weight travelling: **1120kg (2469lb)**	Armour: **n/a**
Weight in action: **unknown**	Engine: **n/a**
Elevation arc: **-5° to +37°**	Muzzle velocity: **680mps (2231fps)**
Traverse arc: **54°**	Speed: **n/a**

SU-76

SPECIFICATIONS

SU-76

Type:
medium SP AT gun

Effective ceiling:
n/a

Calibre:
n/a

Road range:
355km (221 miles)

Vehicle length:
5.03m (16ft 6in)

Range:
n/a

Length of barrel:
n/a

Projectile weight:
n/a

Weight travelling:
n/a

Armour:
15–25mm (.59–1in)

Weight in action:
10,990kg (24,228lb)

Engine:
two GAZ 202

Elevation arc:
n/a

Muzzle velocity:
n/a

Traverse arc:
n/a

Speed:
45km/h (28mph)

Appreciating the urgent need for a weapon to defeat German vehicles such as the PzKpfw III and PzKpfw IV tanks, the Soviets rightly decided that in the short term their best bet lay with the installation of a powerful gun on a light chassis to create a nimble yet hard-hitting tank destroyer that could be developed quickly and placed in production early enough to help stem the German invasion.

Such a weapon entered service in 1942 as the four-man 76mm Self-Propelled Gun (SU-76). This was essentially the 76.2mm Model 1942/SiS-3 gun mounted in a fixed armoured superstructure on a lengthened T-70 light tank chassis. However, the increasing armour thickness of German tanks soon combined with the vulnerability deriving from its own thin armour to make the SU-76 better suited to the infantry support role.

The gun could fire HE, APHE, HVAP and HEAT rounds at muzzle velocities between 325 and 965m (1065 and 3167ft) per second, and carried 60 mixed rounds for the gun that could be elevated in an arc between -3° and +25°, and traversed 32°. An improved model, the SU-76M with two uprated GAZ-203 engines, and armour protection over the fighting compartment, appeared late in the war. The vehicle performed well in combat.

85MM AA GUN 1944

By the later 1930s the Soviets had become keenly aware that their standard medium anti-aircraft gun, the 76.2mm Model 1931, was scarcely up to the task of tackling and defeating modern warplanes operating at altitude. A major upgrade programme was launched, the first two weapons to appear being the 76.2mm Anti-aircraft Gun Model 1938 that was a significantly updated development of the Model 1931, and the 85mm Anti-aircraft Gun Model 1939 (the specifications for which are listed in the table at right). This latter was basically a scaled-up development of the Model 1938 weapon and was alternatively known as the KS-12. It was a very capable weapon.

By 1939 all Soviet guns were being designed as dual-role weapons with a major anti-tank capability, and this made it feasible later to employ variants of the weapon as the armament of the SU-85 tank destroyer/assault gun and the T-34/85 medium tank.

The Germans used captured weapons with the designation 8.5cm FlaK M.39(r): in common with other captured Soviet guns many were rebored, in this instance to become 8.5/8.8cm FlaK M.39(r) weapons. The 85mm Anti-aircraft Gun Model 1944, or KS-18, was a refined version of the Model 1939 with changes to the recoil mechanism to cater for a more powerful propellant load.

SPECIFICATIONS

85MM AA GUN 1944

Type: **medium towed AA gun**	Effective ceiling: **10,500m (34,450ft)**
Calibre: **85mm (3.346in)**	Road range: **n/a**
Vehicle length: **n/a**	Range: **n/a**
Length of barrel: **4.693m (184.76in)**	Projectile weight: **9.2kg (20.29lb)**
Weight travelling: **4220kg (9303lb)**	Armour: **n/a**
Weight in action: **3060kg (6746lb)**	Engine: **n/a**
Elevation arc: **-2° to +82°**	Muzzle velocity: **800mps (2625fps)**
Traverse arc: **360°**	Speed: **n/a**

SU-85

SPECIFICATIONS

SU-85

Type:
heavy SP AT gun

Calibre:
n/a

Vehicle length:
8.15m (26ft 9in)

Length of barrel:
n/a

Weight travelling:
n/a

Weight in action:
29,600kg (65,256lb)

Elevation arc:
n/a

Traverse arc:
n/a

Effective ceiling:
n/a

Road range:
400km (249 miles)

Range:
n/a

Projectile weight:
n/a

Armour:
20–45mm (.79–1.77in)

Engine:
one Model V-2-34

Muzzle velocity:
n/a

Speed:
50km/h (31mph)

Introduced to service in 1943, the 85mm Self-Propelled Gun, generally known as the SU-85, was developed in haste as a powerful tank destroyer to combat the latest German tanks, the PzKpfw V Panther medium and PzKpfw VI Tiger heavy vehicles that were appearing in increasing numbers on the Eastern Front.

The four-man SU-85 was of typical Soviet self-propelled gun configuration and based on the chassis of the classic T-34 medium tank. This was revised with a fighting compartment over the forward part of the hull in place of the turret, and this fighting compartment was of sloped armour including a large front plate. The first SU-85 vehicles had an unsophisticated cupola over the fighting compartment, but a more advanced cupola was introduced later in the war. Provided with 48 rounds of ammunition, the 85mm gun was the D-S85 (later D-5S) adaptation of the high-velocity Anti-aircraft Gun Model 1939, and this was an L/52 weapon firing two types of ammunition: APHE and HVAP types with muzzle velocities of 790 and 1030m (2592 and 3379ft) per second respectively. To maintain its capability against German tanks as armour thickness increased, the basic vehicle was later developed into the SU-100 with a 100mm Model 1944 (D-10S) gun. This vehicle was a potent tank killer.

100MM ANTI-TANK GUN 1944

Unlike a number of other countries, which stepped up from light/medium-calibre anti-tank guns in 57mm calibre or similar to large-calibre guns via the intermediate stage of weapons with a calibre in the order of 75mm, the Soviets opted to omit this stage and move straight from the 57mm calibre to a heavy weapon of 100mm calibre. This resulted in the 100mm Anti-Tank Gun Model 1944 that was certainly one of the finest weapons of its type to see service in World War II, and took a heavy toll of German armour during the titanic tank battles on the Eastern Front in the later stages of the war.

The gun was derived from a piece of naval ordnance, like all weapons of its type designed for a high muzzle velocity and therefore a flat trajectory, and installed on a heavy carriage of the split-trail type with a small but effective shield with slightly backward-angled side sections, and a single axle carrying two pairs of pneumatically tyred wheels. The weapon was fitted with a double-baffle muzzle brake and possessed a well-designed breech that contributed to the excellent maximum fire rate of between 8 and 10 rounds per minute. The maximum range was 21,000m (22,965 yards), and the armour penetration of its heavy projectile was very good.

SPECIFICATIONS

100MM ANTI-TANK GUN 1944

Type: **heavy towed AT gun**	Effective ceiling: **n/a**
Calibre: **100mm (3.94in)**	Road range: **n/a**
Vehicle length: **n/a**	Range: **21,000m (22,965 yards)**
Length of barrel: **5.97m (235in)**	Projectile weight: **15.6kg (34.4lb)**
Weight travelling: **n/a**	Armour: **n/a**
Weight in action: **3460kg (7628lb)**	Engine: **n/a**
Elevation arc: **-5° to +45°**	Muzzle velocity: **900mps (2952fps)**
Traverse arc: **58**	Speed: **n/a**

SU-100

SPECIFICATIONS

SU-100

Type: **heavy SP AT gun**	Effective ceiling: **n/a**
Calibre: **n/a**	Road range: **320km (200 miles)**
Vehicle length: **9.45m (31ft)**	Range: **n/a**
Length of barrel: **n/a**	Projectile weight: **n/a**
Weight travelling: **31,600kg (69,665lb)**	Armour: **20–54mm (.79–2.13in)**
Weight in action: **n/a**	Engine: **Model V-2-34**
Elevation arc: **n/a**	Muzzle velocity: **n/a**
Traverse arc: **n/a**	Speed: **48km/h (30mph)**

Otherwise known as the SU-100, the 100mm Self-Propelled Gun was the last of the USSR's tank destroyers to be based on the chassis of the T-34 medium tank, and was a four-man equipment that entered service in 1944 to give the Soviet Army a weapon capable of defeating the latest German tanks but maintaining an edge on performance and agility over its opponents. The SU-100 was derived fairly closely from the SU-85, and thus had its engine at the rear and, in place of the tank's rotating turret, a forward firing compartment made of well-sloped armour.

The gun, which protruded through the front plate slightly to the right of the centreline (with a large mantlet to protect the aperture) alongside the driver's hatch, was the 100mm Model 1944 (otherwise D-10S) high-velocity weapon. This long-barrel gun was the same ordnance as later carried by the T-54 tank, and was supplied with 34 rounds of mixed HVAP and APHE ammunition: the 19.5kg (43lb) HVAP round left the muzzle at 1000m (3281ft) per second, while the 16kg (35.3kg) APHE round left the muzzle at 920m (3018ft) per second and possessed a maximum range of 19,200m (20,995 yards). The gun could be elevated in an arc between -2° to +17°. It could knock out all but the heaviest German tanks.

122MM FIELD GUN A-19

The 122mm Field Gun Model 1931 marked an important step in the modernization of the Soviet Army's artillery arm, and combined a new barrel with an existing carriage, that of the 152mm Gun/Howitzer Model 1934 introduced to service at about the same time. The Model 1931 (or 122-31) was a completely orthodox but highly effective weapon of great reliability, and the Germans used captured examples with the designation 12.2cm Kanone 390/1(r). During 1937 the Model 1931's barrel was mounted on the carriage of the 152mm Gun/Howitzer Model 1937 to become the Model 1931/37 (otherwise 122-31/37 or A-19).

This updated model differed in appearance from its parent only in the rearward rather than forward slope of the equilibrators on each side of the barrel.

The Germans operated this version of the 122mm gun as the 12.2cm Kanone 390/2(r) and, as was the case with the K 390/1(r), shifted significant numbers to the West for inclusion in their "Atlantic Wall" defences of France, where they totally failed to prevent the Allied invasion or inflict serious damage on the forces that poured ashore on D-Day. The A-19S version of the later gun was carried in the SU-122 heavy tank destroyer, where it gave good service against the depleted units of Hitler's panzer divisions.

SPECIFICATIONS

122MM FIELD GUN A-19

Type: **heavy towed gun**	Effective ceiling: **n/a**
Calibre: **121.92mm (4.8in)**	Road range: **n/a**
Vehicle length: **n/a**	Range: **20,870m (22,825 yards)**
Length of barrel: **5.483m (215.86in)**	Projectile weight: **25kg (55.1lb)**
Weight travelling: **7800kg (17,196lb)**	Armour: **n/a**
Weight in action: **7100kg (15,653lb)**	Engine: **n/a**
Elevation arc: **-4° to +45°**	Muzzle velocity: **800mps (2625fps)**
Traverse arc: **56°**	Speed: **n/a**

SU-122

SPECIFICATIONS

SU-122

Type:
heavy SP AT gun

Calibre:
n/a

Vehicle length:
9.80m (32ft 2in)

Length of barrel:
n/a

Weight travelling:
44,350kg (97,773lb)

Weight in action:
n/a

Elevation arc:
n/a

Traverse arc:
n/a

Effective ceiling:
n/a

Road range:
340km (211 miles)

Range:
n/a

Projectile weight:
n/a

Armour:
22–75mm (.87–2.95in)

Engine:
one Model V-2-K

Muzzle velocity:
n/a

Speed:
45km/h (28mph)

The 122mm Self-Propelled Gun, usually known by the SU-122 abbreviation of its full Soviet designation, should not be confused with an identically designated self-propelled assault gun based on the chassis of the T-34 medium tank. The intention of the design programme, which was initiated during 1943, was the creation of the most powerful possible tank destroyer on the basis of an existing tank chassis, that of the KV heavy tank. First thoughts were centred on the use of the KV-2 with the 122mm Model 1944 (D-25S) gun in the turret, but then the attraction of the standard tank destroyer configuration (fixed fighting compartment with a limited-traverse gun) became too strong to ignore, and the four-man SU-122 appeared in 1944 with a rear-mounted engine and forward-set fighting compartment of well-sloped armour.

A feature of Soviet armoured fighting vehicles was their lack of space for ammunition. The SU-122 was no different: it had 25 rounds of ammunition, the 122mm Model 1931–37 gun was offset slightly to the right of the centreline and emerged from the front plate via an aperture protected by a large mantlet. Only 100 of these large equipments had been completed before production switched to the ISU-122 based on the chassis of the more advanced Josef Stalin heavy tank.

152MM FIELD GUN BR-2

The 152mm Field Gun Model 1935, otherwise known as the 152-35 or BR-2, remains an obscure weapon about which little reliable information has ever become available. The type was clearly intended for the counter-battery role in succession to the obsolescent 152mm Field Gun Model 1910/30. There were evidently fears that so massive a weapon would lack adequate mobility across country as well as on many of the USSR's unpaved roads, which became mud tracks in the autumn rains and spring thaws, so the type was installed on a carriage with caterpillar tracks rather than wheels (it is a misconception that the Soviets were unaffected by the mud and snow on the Eastern Front; their troops and vehicles got just as stuck as those of the enemy, and many Red Army winter offensives failed because the heavy artillery pieces could not be moved forward in the deep snow and/or mud). Stability in the firing position was aided by the use of a split-trail arrangement, and this was reflected in moderately good accuracy to a considerable range. Only a comparatively small number of these powerful gun/howitzer equipments was manufactured, and although the type was accorded the German designation 15.2cm Kanone 440(r) there is no evidence that any of the type were ever used by the Germans after being captured.

SPECIFICATIONS

152MM FIELD GUN BR-2

Type: **heavy gun/howitzer**	Effective ceiling: **n/a**
Calibre: **152.4mm (6in)**	Road range: **n/a**
Vehicle length: **n/a**	Range: **27,000m (29,530 yards)**
Length of barrel: **7.62m (300in)**	Projectile weight: **48.5kg (106.9lb)**
Weight travelling: **n/a**	Armour: **n/a**
Weight in action: **18,200kg (40,123lb)**	Engine: **n/a**
Elevation arc: **0° to +60°**	Muzzle velocity: **880mps (2887fps)**
Traverse arc: **8°**	Speed: **n/a**

152MM HOWITZER ML-20

SPECIFICATIONS

152MM HOWITZER ML-20

Type: **heavy gun/howitzer**	Effective ceiling: **n/a**
Calibre: **152.4mm (6in)**	Road range: **n/a**
Vehicle length: **n/a**	Range: **17,250m (18,865 yards)**
Length of barrel: **4.404m (173.4in)**	Projectile weight: **43.56kg (96.03lb)**
Weight travelling: **7930kg (17,482lb)**	Armour: **n/a**
Weight in action: **7130kg (15,719lb)**	Engine: **n/a**
Elevation arc: **-2° to +65°**	Muzzle velocity: **655mps (2149fps)**
Traverse arc: **58°**	Speed: **n/a**

The 152mm Gun/Howitzer Model 1937, generally known as the 152–37 and later as the ML–20, was vital to Soviet counter-battery efforts in World War II and, in common with many other effective Soviet weapons, was something of a hybrid. The Red Army viewed artillery as being the God of War, and in this weapon it possessed pieces that could be considered to be among the major deities.

The equipment thus comprised the barrel of the 152mm Gun/Howitzer Model 1910/34r on versions of the carriage initially created for the 122mm Field Gun Model 1931/37: one carriage had spoked wheels and was intended for horse traction, while the other had tyred double steel wheels for motor traction. In each case the equipment was towed as a single load. The success of the combination is attested by the very large number of weapons that were completed, and the power of this weapon fire is also suggested by the fact that the ML-20S version of the gun was used in the SU-152 and ISU-152 heavy assault guns. The Germans were highly impressed with the weapon and used captured examples with the designation 15.2cm Kanonehaubitze 433/l(r), often emplaced in coastal defences. Ironically, they were largely wasted in such places, but they looked good on propaganda newsreels.

203MM HOWITZER B-4

The 203mm Howitzer Model 1931 was a very distinctive piece of heavy artillery, most notably for its employment of a tracked rather than wheeled carriage and also for the fact that the weapon was produced in no fewer than six variants (known only by their German designations 20.3cm Haubitze 503[r] to 503/5[r]) all transported in two loads. These variants differed from each other in their type of barrel carriage and the carriage's suspension: the first five variants had a wheeled transporter (different wheel sizes) for the barrel, while the sixth had a tracked transporter. Moreover, the first and last three variants had an L/22 and L/25 barrel respectively, and it is thought that most of the earlier weapons were later refitted with the average L/25 ordnance.

The first variant fired a 98kg (216.05lb) shell to 12800m (14,000 yards), but the others fired a heavier shell to a somewhat longer range. It appears that the last such weapons were delivered in 1937, and the Germans used captured examples of these powerful pieces of artillery (only the last three variants with the longer barrel) only on the Eastern Front against their erstwhile owners. By all acounts they performed well, and their tracks provided them with good mobility in a theatre that was notorious for its poor roads.

SPECIFICATIONS

203MM HOWITZER B-4

Type: **heavy towed howitzer**	Effective ceiling: **n/a**
Calibre: **203.2mm (8in)**	Road range: **n/a**
Vehicle length: **n/a**	Range: **16,000m (17,500 yards)**
Length of barrel: **4.915m (193.53in)**	Projectile weight: **100kg (220.5lb)**
Weight travelling: **n/a**	Armour: **n/a**
Weight in action: **17,700kg (39,021lb)**	Engine: **n/a**
Elevation arc: **0° to +60°**	Muzzle velocity: **610mps (2001fps)**
Traverse arc: **8°**	Speed: **n/a**

INDEX